A GUIDE TO
WESTERN BIRD FEEDING

A GUIDE TO
WESTERN BIRD FEEDING

by John V. Dennis

Foreword by
Kenn Kaufman

Illustrations by
Dimitry Schidlovsky

Bird Watcher's Digest Press

Other Books by John V. Dennis

A Complete Guide to Bird Feeding (1975)

World Guide to Tropical Drift Seeds and Fruits (1976)
with Dr. C. R. Gunn

Beyond the Bird Feeder (1981)

The Wildlife Gardener (1985)

The Great Cypress Swamps (1988)

Summer Bird Feeding (1988)

Table of Contents

Foreword

On this December afternoon, our windowsill is decked with an array of Christmas cards. Because Lynn and I are both bird watchers, and because all our friends know it, most of the cards carry pictures of birds. A frequent theme is "The Birds' Christmas," with a colorful party of songbirds clustered around a bird feeder. This scene is repeated a dozen times: cardinals, blue jays, purple finches, chickadees, white-throated sparrows, tufted titmice, American goldfinches, and other backyard favorites, enjoying their holiday feast of suet and seeds.

If I raise my eyes from the card collection and look out the window, I see a real-life version of the same picture—almost. The scene is the same, but the cast of characters is different. Instead of the cardinal there is another crested bird, the pyrrhuloxia. In place of the white-throated sparrows, there are white-crowned sparrows. The purple finches and American goldfinches are replaced by house finches and lesser goldfinches. Blue jays and tufted titmice are nowhere to be seen, but canyon towhees and verdins are making themselves conspicuous.

Why is the reality at this bird feeder so different from the image on the cards? Because this feeder is in Tucson, Arizona. This feeder is in the West.

Feeding wild birds is now a tremendously popular activity in North America. Much has been published on the subject, in books, magazines, mail-order catalogs, and yes, greeting cards—but most of this material is slanted toward eastern readers and eastern birds. This eastern bias would have been logical at the beginning of the 20th century, when most bird feeders were between the Atlantic and the Mississippi. Today, it no longer makes sense. Bird feeding has come of age in the West. Towns in the Rockies bristle with hummingbird feeders in summer and suet feeders in winter. Desert suburbanites put out seeds for their quail and doves and finches. Feeders near the Mexican border draw such exotic creatures as green jays and bridled titmice, while feeders in northern montane valleys may be drained in winter by swirling flocks of rosy finches. Hummingbird feeders along the Pacific Coast and in the Southwest are patronized year-round. Altogether, feeders in the West are likely to attract more kinds of birds than feeders in the East.

And that may be part of the problem. In terms of bird habitats, the West is complex. It is a land of extremes. The West has elevations that are both lower (well below sea level) and much higher than anything east of the Great Plains. The West has climates that are hotter and colder, wetter and drier, more variable and more constant, than any in the East. And the bird life varies just as dramatically. In the East, from Milwaukee to Memphis, from Birmingham to Boston, many of the feeder birds are the same. In the West, birds at a feeder in an arid valley might be totally different from those in a mountain forest ten miles away.

Greater contrasts make for greater variety. East of the Mississippi, only one species of hummingbird can be expected; west of it, there are at least 15. The West has more different kinds of chickadees, goldfinches, juncos, orioles, towhees, jays . . . more feeder birds in general. Perhaps many writers focus on bird feeding in the East because the West is too complicated.

Undaunted by the challenge, however, is John V. Dennis, a renowned authority on the techniques of attracting wildlife. He knows his topics from A to Z, but as his writing reveals, he still finds it exciting; he writes with the zest of a newcomer and the knowledge of a seasoned expert. John Dennis has done research on bird feeding throughout the continent; his network of contacts, many made through *Bird Watcher's Digest*, adds another dimension to his storehouse of information. In this book he presents everything you need to know about feeding the fascinating birds of the West.

—Kenn Kaufman
Tucson, Arizona

Preface

Unlike the East, where feeder birds are much the same wherever feeding is conducted, the West, with its pronounced differences in altitude and climate, offers a richer diversity of birds. Yet little has been written about feeding the birds of this vast area which covers more than half of North America. For decades, as bird watching and bird feeding activity has increased, Westerners have had to wait for field guides and books about western birds, while the bird enthusiasts of the East had many such references from which to choose. This book is designed to serve as a reference for Westerners who already feed birds and for those beginners who want to experience firsthand the wonders of bird feeding.

The West has arid deserts, high mountain ranges and tundra, humid coastal forests, scrubland, prairie, and many other habitat types, each of which supports a different mixture of bird life. But how do these differences in habitat affect the techniques we use to attract and feed the birds? Are the same foods and feeding station techniques universally applicable for feeder birds?

To examine western bird feeding I divided western North America into eight geographical regions and devoted a chapter to the feeder birds of each region. The boundaries of the eight regions, though largely artificial, tend to follow the outstanding geographical features of western North America.

To augment the existing knowledge about bird feeding in the West, I developed a series of questionnaires designed to reach a cross-section of people who feed birds in the western United States and Canada. These questionnaires, along with a good deal of correspondence with experienced feeding station operators from the various regions, supplemented nicely my personal experience in feeding western birds.

For each of the eight regions of the West, I have described several typical feeding stations, the birds they attract, and how these birds are attracted. If you want to know more about feeding birds in your area, the examples cited in the chapter covering your region of the West will give you an idea how others operate their feeding stations and what birds they attract. It is important to note that the examples given are not the only methods of feeding that will work. Experiment with new foods and styles of feeding the birds in your area. You may be surprised at what you discover about your feeder visitors.

My thanks for help received in completing this book go, first of all, to my editor, Bill Thompson, III, and to my other good friends at *Bird Watcher's Digest*, Mary Beacom Bowers, William (Jr.) and Elsa Thompson, Pat Murphy, Terry Nutter, Martha Wilson, and Brady Peery. Their interest in this project, and that of Tom Post of Audubon Workshop, was instrumental in getting me started. John Johanek and his staff at Publication Design contributed greatly to the production of this book

Kenn Kaufman, in Tucson, Arizona, offered many helpful comments on a final draft of the manuscript, in addition to writing the book's foreword, for which I am very grateful. My thanks, also, to Erica H. Dunn of Project FeederWatch for her contributions on the feeder surveys in Chapter 12.

In addition, my gratitude to all the many persons who have assisted by responding to questionnaires, correspondence, or by critically reading portions of the manuscript. Especially helpful were: Monica and William Heath in Alaska; William A. Davis, Jerome J. Pratt, and Sally H. Spofford in Arizona; Judith K. Berg, Nancy Kelly, Mrs. Michael Kew, John F. Walters, and Margaret West in California; Stephen Frye and Katherine F. Spahn in Colorado; Mrs. Wayne Eveland in Montana; Greg Scyphers in Nevada; Judith Fishback, Ralph A. Fisher, Jr., and Natalie Owings in New Mexico; John Skeen and Luann Waters in Oklahoma; James Davis, Virginia Holmgren, Sally Spaulding, and Herbert Wisner in Oregon; Betty and Dan Baker, Rose Farmer, Jesse Grantham, Kay McCracken, Hans J. Mueller, and Barry R. Zimmer in Texas; Jewell A. Gifford in Utah; Thero North and Jeanette Urbain in Washington; and Barbara Wise in Wyoming.

Thanks also to Brian Self and R. Wayne Campbell in British Columbia, Jean Bancroft in Manitoba, and Ernie Kuyt in Saskatchewan.

Dedication

To my good friend Howard A. Winkler of Tucson, Arizona, who kindled my interest in birds and bird watching when, many years ago, we were students at the University of Wisconsin.

—John V. Dennis
May 1, 1991

Chapter 1

A HISTORY OF
WESTERN BIRD FEEDING

Early attempts to feed hummingbirds looked something like this.

Long before the days of bird foods and specially made feeders, Westerners were using improvised methods to attract birds to their campsites or dwellings. One of the earliest accounts was by William Scott, who in an 1886 issue of the ornithological journal *The Auk*, told of feeding gray-breasted jays in Arizona. He simply hung a piece of meat or meat bone in a tree near his home and watched the jays as they came in to feed.

Around 1890, in a California garden, a young girl convalescing from an illness conducted the first experiments we know of in attracting hummingbirds. First using a tubular flower of the kind hummingbirds were visiting and then the same flower filled with a sugar water solution, she was able to bring Anna's hummingbirds in to feed as she held the flower in her hand. She conducted her experiments while relaxing in a chair, basking in the warm sunshine.

By 1900, people were using small glass vials filled with sweet solutions to attract hummingbirds. These feeders were hung out-of-doors where the hummingbirds could be watched from a convenient vantage point. From these simple beginnings, hummingbird feeding developed into the art that it is today. Gradually, through trial and error, people learned there were good and bad ways to feed hummingbirds.

In the western mountains, birds were so forward about coming to food that they needed no special invitation. They boldly flew into campsites to search for scraps and would even enter tents and cabins. There was no such thing as hiding food from gray jays and Clark's nutcrackers, which would swoop by to seize a morsel from a frying pan or even the plate from which one was eating. Often the only solution seemed to be to offer the birds food before they pilfered it. But the primary reason that people fed birds in the wilderness was for the amusement and companionship they provided. Perhaps the backwoods seemed a little less lonely when birds appeared almost as soon as a campfire was lighted.

Guests at hotels and lodges enjoyed the birds as much as did backwoodsmen and campers. William L. Finley, a well-known ornithologist and bird photographer, told how birds offered entertainment to guests at the Cloud Cap Inn high on the north slope of Mount Hood in Oregon. He described guests watching the nutcrackers and gray jays that came in to eat table scraps. The guests enjoyed these birds as much as they did the spectacular view. Bird feeding at the Cloud Cap seems to have been initiated around 1900. Similarly, at the Cragmore, a mountain resort hotel near Colorado Springs, Colorado, daily offerings of table scraps were placed on feeding shelves for birds, for the entertainment of guests. First to come each morning were handsome Steller's jays. They reportedly dominated the feeders until they had had their fill.

It didn't take long to learn that birds visiting feeders were good subjects for bird photography. Some of the earliest feeder photos were taken by Earl R. Forrest, who lived at Oracle, a small town in Arizona, north of Tucson. A photograph taken in 1903 of gray-breasted (then called Arizona) jays at his feeder appeared in Arthur Cleveland Bent's series *Life Histories of North American Birds*, as did one taken the same year of a Gila woodpecker at his feeder.

Another Arizonan, M. French Gilman, was more interested in conducting experiments to see what foods birds at his feeders would eat. His well-stocked bird tables were visited by Gila woodpeckers, mockingbirds, Bendire's and curve-billed thrashers, cactus wrens, brown-headed cowbirds, cardinals, and Abert's towhees. The Gila woodpeckers were omnivorous, eating both meat and seeds or fruit. They were especially fond of meat scraps and ate almost everything else that was offered except pickled olives! Sliced watermelon was a favorite with nearly all the birds. An account of Mr. Gilman's feeding experiments appeared in a 1915 issue of *The Condor*.

Perhaps no one made more use of bird feeders as a place to study birds during this period than Florence Merriam Bailey. Daughter of the distinguished naturalist C. Hart Merriam, she began studying birds as a young woman in the East, but by the turn of the century was spending more and more time in the West. Her special interest was in the habits and behavior of birds. By attracting them with food offerings, she was able to observe details that she would have missed in the field. Her husband, Vernon Bailey, was a government biologist who shared her interests. The two, often camping out, spent years studying the flora and fauna of the Southwest. Mrs. Bailey never neglected an opportunity to bring birds to their tent or cabin with the help of food and water. She wrote so enthusiastically about feeding birds that one gets the impression that bird feeding was as much a source of pleasure to her as it was an opportunity to learn about birds. Even the erudite ornithological publication *The Auk* carried articles by her on the joys of bird feeding in the West. Her two most important works were *Handbook of Birds of the Western United States* published in 1902 and *Birds of New Mexico* published in 1928. Florence M. Bailey's writings did much to increase interest in western birds and in feeding them.

Feeding Gulls and Waterfowl

It is hard to believe that a hundred years ago gulls were so mistrustful of humans that they kept a safe distance from us. But this suddenly began to change as preparations for the Panama-Pacific International Exposition got underway in San Francisco in 1916. Workers, seeing gulls streaming in from San Francisco Bay to pick up scraps, began feeding them. Their example was followed by the throngs of visitors who came to view the exhibits. Becoming ever more confident, the gulls bathed in fountains, congregated on lawns, and barely got out of the way when people walked near them. Gulls, including the ring-billed, western, California, and glaucous-winged, were on hand, as well as coots and Canada geese—all taking advantage of the food that was so easy to obtain.

As in the case of domestic pigeons, some people like gulls and enjoy feeding them; others would rather not have them around. Liked or not, the gulls are making themselves ever more at home in West Coast cities. They patrol the streets, parks, and even tall buildings in downtown sections, searching for sources of food.

Waterfowl also have adapted in certain ways to take advantage of food supplied by humans. A few miles east of the former exposition grounds in San Francisco is Lake Merritt in the heart of the city of Oakland. This lake, a waterfowl sanctuary since 1869, is a gathering place for large numbers of waterfowl during the fall and winter. Some are diving ducks which arrive from San Francisco Bay and others are shovelers, mallards, pintails, and American wigeon which are more closely associated with fresh water. The birds flock in to feed upon grain supplied by the city and bakery products and popcorn supplied by residents. Since Lake Merritt is a saltwater arm of the Bay, the birds need fresh water for drinking purposes. This is supplied to them in shallow cement basins.

Waterfowl have perhaps been fed for a longer period of time here than anywhere else in the West. The lake with its feeding program has served as a model for other towns and cities in the West.

Mallards, pintails, and shovelers dabbling in a city park pond.

Without the help of artificial feeding, waterfowl would not have sufficient food to attract and maintain wintering populations in protected areas such as Lake Merritt. There is little in the way of natural food in cities where most of the feeding is conducted. But it is important that the example set by Lake Merritt be followed and that whole grain, such as corn, wheat, oats, and sorghum, be supplied along with the foods offered by residents.

Better Feeders for Hummingbirds

In 1926, a banker and philanthropist named B. F. Tucker decided that he would do something to build up the hummingbird population around his home in southern California. He and his wife lived in Modjeska Canyon, a beautiful oak-clad stream valley near the city of Orange. Although as many as six species of hummingbirds visited the canyon—some of them present in winter and others migrants—few, if any, were seen during the long summer dry season. The birds disappeared about the time the flowers they depended upon for nectar wilted. Would artificial feeding hold nesting species through the summer?

Using simple glass tube type feeders with red ribbons attached to them, Mr. Tucker was able to induce a few Anna's hummingbirds to spend the summer. But he soon discovered that the honey solution he was using attracted too many bees and so he switched to a sugar water formula. (As we shall see, honey has a number of drawbacks as a hummingbird food and shouldn't be used.) Next, Mr. Tucker switched to larger feeders of his own design that could accommodate as many as eight hummers at a time. The feeder was an up-ended glass bottle over a bowl containing openings through which the birds could drink. Perches allowed the birds to feed without having to hover. Solution was held in the bottle through capillary action (the surface tension of the liquid solution across the small openings is sufficient to prevent it from running out of the bottle). Most hummingbird feeders used today operate in the same manner.

After a few years, there were so many hummingbirds visiting the property that during peak seasons as many as 28 feeders were needed to accommodate them. They were suspended in a row from eaves over the veranda on the shady side of the house. Here, the Tuckers could sit and watch the exciting spectacle of dozens of hummingbirds in view at one time, while a short distance away other birds visited feeders for quail and songbirds.

In 1939, Mr. Tucker deeded the property to the California

Audubon Society. Maintained as a bird sanctuary open to the public, it allowed visitors to observe hummingbird feeding at its best. Feeders designed by Mr. Tucker could be bought at the sanctuary or ordered through the mail. Mr. Tucker had had his wish of bringing more hummingbirds to his home and through the example of his feeding experiments, he helped numerous others do the same. When I visited the Tucker Sanctuary in the spring of 1958, I had the satisfaction of sitting on the veranda and watching, as had the Tuckers, an endless stream of hummingbirds coming to the feeders.

Gray jays are brazen about getting food from humans. Early Westerners called them "camp robbers."

Bird Feeding Today

As we have seen, bird feeding in the West had simple beginnings in the mountains, along the coast, and in towns and cities. It caught the fancy of people partly because the birds were so easy to attract and so interesting to watch. There is also a deep-seated sentimentality in nearly all of us. We want to feed almost any animal that seems at all hungry. Besides the pleasure and companionship that bird feeding offers, it has practical advantages for studying food habits and behavior, and for bird photography. Having birds close by where they can be viewed and identified easily is also a wonderful way to learn about birds, but it is also very enjoyable.

In the last few decades more and more people have been feeding birds in the West. In some areas, few yards are without bird feeders. With increased participation, the trend is toward better feeders and feeding methods. Most people now buy feeders and bird foods from suppliers, which has made for more uniformity in how birds are fed. But there is still room for experimenting on one's own. Somewhat different methods apply in different parts of the West, which is why in this book we examine bird feeding in the West on a regional basis. Something that suits birds in the humid Pacific Northwest may not apply in the desertlike Southwest.

Wherever feeding is conducted, care should be taken to look after all the small details that go into making it a success. Nowhere is this more important than in feeding hummingbirds. In the next chapter, we provide more information about these dazzling small birds so common in parts of the West and tell how best to attract and feed them. ☐

Chapter 2

FEEDING HUMMINGBIRDS

An Allen's hummingbird.

F ew New World birds have captured as much attention as the hummingbirds. The early Spanish endowed hummingbirds with mystical qualities and were sometimes confused as to whether they were birds or insects. It is true that hummingbirds have an insectlike quality to them. Like bees and sphinx moths, they dart from flower to flower sipping nectar from each one they visit. Hummingbirds also carry pollen inadvertently to other flowers and therefore serve as pollinators. Their extraordinary ability to fly forward or backward, hover in midair, shift sideways, fly straight up or down, and suddenly stop in mid-flight also reminds us of insects, as does their apparent fearlessness in the presence of humans. But a closer look reveals feathers, not scales, and a bill instead of a proboscis. This tells us we are looking at a hummingbird.

With a rate of metabolism higher than that of any other avian species, hummingbirds have to eat a lot and eat at frequent intervals. It has been reported that some Brazilian species consume 30 times their own weight in food in a day! Hummingbirds do their heaviest feeding early in the morning after they leave their nighttime roosts, and again before returning near dusk. Under adverse conditions, such as very low temperatures, hummers may go into a torpor or state of dormancy. At such times all bodily functions slow almost to a stop. No longer expending energy, the bird can get along for a time without eating. With the return of sunshine after a cold night, the torpid bird quickly recovers and its metabolism returns to normal.

Hummingbirds have a specialized diet, necessary to satisfy their high metabolic rate. They require both an energy-giving liquid, usually flower nectar (though some species also consume tree sap from woodpecker holes), and protein, which they get by eating small insects, spiders, and daddy longlegs.

Bill length is a clue to what hummingbirds eat. Those with very long, and often pronouncedly decurved bills are dominantly nectar feeders. The bill, by its shape and size, is well adapted for the deep probing of the flowers the birds most often visit. Species with very short bills are primarily insect feeders. Those with intermediate bill lengths, which includes the species recorded north of Mexico, take both nectar and insects in somewhere near equal amounts. The flowers they most often visit are likely to be bright in color (often red or orange), funnel-shaped, and easy to reach by fluttering before them on rapidly beating wings. These garden and wildflower species (generically called hummingbird flowers), typically have no fragrance. They evolved being pollinated by birds which are attracted by their brightly colored flowers. Fragrance-producing flowers attract bees, butterflies, and moths as primary pollinators. This is not to say that hummingbirds do not visit flowers of other kinds. They do and often in competition with other nectar-feeders.

Since the first attempts were made to feed hummingbirds in the wild about 100 years ago, improved techniques have made it possible to accommodate many hummingbirds at our feeders at one time. People living along well-traveled hummingbird migration routes have learned to expect hundreds of hummingbirds at certain times of the year. Before setting out on the next stage of migration, the birds refuel, drinking incredible amounts of sugar water in a single day. Over time this has called for larger feeders that hold more solution, enough to satisfy the needs of the many hummers. Even with today's modified feeders, in some areas there are so many resident birds coming in to feed that feeder operators have difficulty meeting the demand.

Hummingbirds are not found everywhere in the West. They are largely absent from the barren, open terrain of the central and northern Great Plains. The preferred habitats of hummingbirds include wooded canyons, mountain slopes, and meadows, as well as the cactus, mesquite, sage, and thorny shrub regions at lower elevations. Most species require a source of water nearby before they will nest. Thanks to amenities offered by humans—well-planted yards, flowers, feeders, and water—many species reside in towns and cities and may even show a preference for habitat of this kind over natural habitat.

Hummingbirds enthrall bird watchers, artists, photographers, and all those who take delight in sheer beauty. That such fascinating birds can easily be lured to the yard is the reason why hummingbird feeding has become so popular. There is also the somewhat-justified feeling that we are helping hummingbirds by feeding them. In an Arizona study, it was found that a mountain canyon in summer offered only enough wildflowers to support 1.5 hummers! Yet dozens of the birds frequented feeders in the canyon that provided them with all the "nectar" they needed. Hummingbirds, like other species, will adapt their feeding habits to take full advantage of an available food source.

In some parts of the West, hummingbird feeding is a year-round activity; in other parts feeding begins when the first hummingbirds arrive in the spring and stops only after the last one has departed in the fall. All too often, the flowers the birds depend upon are in short supply. This happens annually wherever the summer is very dry or where habitat loss is severe. As we have seen, it takes a lot of nectar to supply the needs of these very active birds.

Those who feed hummingbirds soon discover that these tiny visitors are not so different from other birds in their yards. They nest, bathe, preen, molt, and migrate as the others do. But hummingbirds also have special characteristics of their own. Beating their wings from 70 to 200 times per second, hummingbirds can hover, stop in midair, fly backwards and upside-down, and change directions in a flash. They will tenaciously defend a

A listing of hummingbird plants can be found on page 185 and in each regional chapter.

feeder or natural source of nectar during the nesting season, and the rufous hummingbird will even establish and defend a feeding territory during migration.

Numbers and Species

In the New World the vast majority of hummingbirds live in the American tropics, stretching from Mexico to Brazil and Peru. Of the more than 340 hummingbird species known (new ones are still being discovered in the tropics), only a relative few spill across our borders to nest while a few others appear as seasonal visitors. Taking into account the 13 species that nest and others that appear from time to time, we can lay claim to part-time presence of only six to seven percent of the hummingbird species found in the Americas. All of the hummers we see in the United States and Canada have ranges that extend southward into Mexico. And, as with most of our songbird species, the majority of the hummingbirds we see and feed spend only the warm months in our midst, migrating to warmer climes during fall and winter.

This does not mean that there is any shortage of hummingbirds on our side of the border. Several of our nesting species, including the Anna's, black-chinned, and broad-tailed, have very wide ranges and large total populations in western North America. And in some areas, hummers are present the entire year, depending on food availability and weather conditions.

But how do we know which hummers might show up at our feeders? In general, our hummingbirds can be divided into geographical groups based on their breeding ranges. Along the West Coast the Anna's, Costa's, black-chinned, rufous, Allen's, and Calliope hummingbirds are the most likely to be found. In the western mountains, at higher elevations, we find the black-chinned, broad-tailed, Calliope, and rufous hummers.

By far the richest area for hummingbirds in northern North America is the Southwest, and in particular the mountain ranges of southwestern New Mexico and southeastern Arizona. In this region, a lucky bird watcher may find all of our breeding hummers, except the ruby-throated and buff-bellied. Fairly common here are Anna's, black-chinned, blue-throated, broad-tailed, broad-billed, Costa's, and magnificent. Several of the exciting Mexican visitors, such as the berylline, Lucifer, violet-crowned, and white-eared, among others, can also be found, especially at busy feeding stations where large numbers of hummers congregate.

The ruby-throated, the only hummingbird with a broad

breeding range east of the Mississippi River, also breeds throughout the southern halves of Manitoba, Saskatchewan, and Alberta in Canada.

In the Northwest, the breeding hummingbirds include Anna's, black-chinned, Calliope, rufous, and ruby-throated (in south-central Canada). While western Canada has these five breeding hummingbird species, only one, the rufous hummingbird, breeds as far north as Alaska. The Anna's continues to spread ever farther north and east of its original west coast range. It is now a resident and breeding in the Vancouver area.

During fall migration, a surprising variety of western hummingbirds pass through southern and south-central Texas, and the coastal region of Louisiana. Many of them spend the winter here. Their appearance is largely a recent phenomenon and we will examine this more closely, later, in the regional chapters.

Identification

Once you have determined which hummingbird species you can expect in your area, the next step is identifying those which visit your yard or feeder. At first glance, proper identification of hummingbirds may seem like a formidable task. In most species the females are far less colorful and less distinctly marked than the males. To further complicate identification, females and immatures (birds less than one year old) look alike. Therefore in some species this leaves us with only the adult male to help us. Luckily his identification is easy if we see him in direct sunlight.

If a nectar feeder has perches, hummers can rest while feeding.

Most bird field guides use the following clues to identify hummingbirds: gorget color of adult males, sound (calls, songs, or wing whistle), size, bill length and color, and general plumage markings. The identification tips below, when used in conjunction with any one of the several field guides available, should make hummingbird identification easier and more enjoyable.

Gorget

One of the best visual clues to a hummer's identity lies in the gorget, or throat patch of the male. The gorget is composed of flat, iridescent feathers which flash a bright color when sunlight is reflected off them at a certain angle. Unless viewed in good light, the true color of the gorget is hard to discern; it may appear to be nothing more than a dark patch. Males use their gorgets in breeding displays to attract mates and in threat displays to drive intruders off their territories.

Gorget colors vary from species to species; green in the magnificent, a ruby-red in the ruby-throated hummingbird, and a violet blue, with greatly elongated side stripes in the Costa's are just three examples. Different colors and design variations are found in our other hummingbirds. Consult your field guide for detailed descriptions of specific species.

Sound

If you have an ear for high-pitched bird calls, sound is a useful clue in identifying hummingbirds. Though most lack a true song, hummingbirds express themselves by uttering distinctive chipping notes either when flying or perched. The more excited the bird is, the louder and more rapid the notes may be. Calls, like gorgets, are frequently used during breeding flight displays and during territorial displays. While the calls of most hummers are short buzzy trills, twitters, and chips, only the male Anna's notes are considered melodious enough to pass as a song. The male Anna's will sing a long series of high buzzes, squeaks, and trills, "suggestive of filing a saw" from a perch on its territory, according to Bent's *Life Histories of North American Birds*. Perhaps it is the duration of this bird's song, rather than the quality, which has earned the Anna's the reputation of being our best singing hummer. The Costa's, blue-throated, and violet-crowned hummers also have vocalizations that function as song.

A second kind of sound comes from the buzzing or whirr of the wings when the bird is in flight, sometimes called the "wing whistle." In adult male broad-tailed hummingbirds the wing

whistle is especially audible and provides a good clue to identifying this species. This sound has been described as a loud, mu-
sical, cricketlike trill. With practice, one can also distinguish the
difference between hummingbird species producing a wing
noise, such as the rufous, Allen's, and black-chinned.

Size

Size can be helpful in identifying hummers, though it can
sometimes be difficult to estimate when the bird in question is
constantly in motion. Hummers on our side of the border range
in length (measured from tip of bill to tip of tail) from five inches
found in the relatively large magnificent and blue-throated
hummingbirds of the Southwest, to the three-and-one-quarter
inch length of the tiny Calliope, North America's smallest bird.
Knowing the relative size of your feeder, a flower stem, or another object regularly visited by a hummer may make estimating
size easier.

Bill Length and Color

Most of our hummingbirds have straight, medium-length
bills. But the Costa's and Calliope have relatively short bills and
the Lucifer has a long, moderately decurved bill. The plain-
capped starthroat, a rare visitor to Arizona from bill Mexico, has
the longest of all—about an inch-and-a-half in length, though the
bird itself is only four-and-a-half inches long!

While most species have a black bill, colorful bills are
present in several hummers. The buff-bellied hummingbird of
South Texas has a bright red-orange bill and the broad-billed of
southeastern Arizona has a colorful red bill. Equally striking are
the bright red, black-tipped bills of the violet-crowned and
white-eared hummers. The former is an uncommon breeding
bird and the latter a rare visitor in southeastern Arizona.

Color and Plumage Patterns

Typically the overall color pattern seen in the hummers is a
metallic green or olive bronze above that contrasts with gray-
ish-white or white on the underside. Two exceptions to this color
scheme are the rufous and Allen's hummingbirds.

The rufous lives up to its name by having rufous colored
plumage everywhere except for an orange-red gorget and white
band below it and greenish wings. Almost identical coloration is
seen in the Allen's hummingbird, a look-alike close relative.
Telling these two species apart, among females and immatures,

is considered impossible unless the bird is in the hand. In males, the Allen's has the all-green back and the rufous has a rufous back, often with some green.

For other species, facial markings and tail color and shape are good hints to a hummingbird's identity. In general, look for those plumage characteristics which are most obvious and you will be better able to discover the identity of almost any hummingbird.

Attracting Hummingbirds

Early interest in hummingbirds centered on keeping them in captivity. In light of the hummingbird's specialized diet, this was difficult. Eventually a fortified sugar water formula suitable for captive birds was developed. Formulas of this kind, however, should not be supplied to wild birds, which can nearly always procure the protein they need on their own.

Attracting hummingbirds to feeders and building up a resident population is a step-by-step process. The most successful feeding stations combine plantings of flowers which attract hummingbirds with careful and timely placement of feeders. Having flowers in bloom and feeders filled and outside when the first hummers arrive may make a yard more attractive to a male looking for a nest site. In California, the Allen's hummingbird arrives as early as late January and is followed in February by the rufous.

A male ruby-throat performs his courtship display flight for a female.

The Anna's, a year-round resident of the West Coast region, may already be nesting when these first early migrants arrive. In the case of the Anna's and other over-wintering species, there is no reason to wait for migrants to arrive to begin your feeding program. Indeed in some parts of the West, year-round feeding is the rule. This occurs in southern portions of New Mexico and Arizona, and along the Pacific Coast as far north as British Columbia!

People who must wait for the return of migrants to begin feeding will want to be in time for major flights northward by black-chinned, broad-tailed, and Calliope hummers in April and May. From late April until late September, feeder attendance will be at its height. With young of the year swelling the population, we may need to add more feeders. Being more curious and less cautious than the parents, the youngsters will examine anything that is brightly colored and will quickly find feeders on their own.

Not everyone has immediate success in attracting hummers.

Sometimes an unfavorable location is to blame; other times there may be fewer hummingbirds present than normal. Like other birds, hummers have good seasons and bad ones. A poor nesting season, losses during migration, and habitat destruction are some of the factors that cause a decline in the bird population. Or perhaps there is a problem with the feeding program. It is important to note that certain rules must be followed if we are to have success in attracting these fascinating birds.

Feeders

Since Mr. Tucker put out his small glass vials, many improvements have been made in hummingbird feeders and their design. Today the basic design consists of a long, clear glass or plastic tube with a nozzle or outlet tube at the bottom. There are dozens of variations on this design, as well as different shapes and sizes, but there is still no such thing as a perfect feeder. Complaints most often heard are that the feeder is not durable, is hard to clean, hard to fill, subject to leakage, and loses the "vacuum" that holds the solution in place.

The main consideration when buying a commercial feeder is that it can be easily cleaned and filled, since this is essential to the success of your feeding operation. A dirty feeder will make your solution spoil more quickly, and this will discourage the hummingbirds, and may even harm them. Perhaps the very worst feeders are the ceramic ones that, while attractive to look at, can't be cleaned at all!

If you are just beginning to feed hummers, start with a small feeder. Once you are successful in attracting hummingbirds you may wish to increase your offerings with additional or larger feeders containing more solution.

Sally Spofford, who feeds hummers in southeastern Arizona, has enjoyed success, as many others have, with home-made feeders used along with commercial feeders. Her own versions include such oddities as guinea pig, hamster, or poultry watering bottles, and open cup glass jars about three inches wide and two-and-a-half inches deep. The latter, she finds, are useful for feeding sugar water to other birds and to mammals (many species besides hummingbirds are fond of sugar water). These open vessels are also better suited for hummers with injured bills or tongues.

Mrs. Spofford is ideally situated for large-scale feeding of hummingbirds. She and her husband live in a wooded canyon with a rushing stream at the eastern edge of Arizona's Chiricahua Mountains. No other part of the country offers a greater variety or number of hummingbirds coming to feeders at one time. Over the years, the Spoffords have played host to no fewer than 12 species. During April and September, the busiest months, she has more than 20 feeders in operation and supplies as much as two gallons of sugar water solution in a day!

Placing Feeders

It is best to place feeders where they are protected from wind and, if possible, from direct sunlight. A feeder that can be easily blown by the wind will not only spill solution, it will make it difficult for hummers to get at the sugar water without expending a great deal of energy. A somewhat shady location will help to prevent overly rapid spoilage of the solution in hot weather. Achieving these two goals will save you a lot of time in cleaning and filling your feeders.

Feeders should be placed where they can be readily seen by both hummingbirds and humans. It may help to place your feeders near flowers already favored by the hummers if they have not yet discovered your feeders. Hummer feeders can be suspended from almost any convenient place—a clothesline, the eaves of the house, the limb of a shrub or tree. It is easiest to fill and maintain them when they are hung in a row, a few feet apart. Sometimes such an arrangement works out very nicely, but if an overly aggressive male is bent upon chasing every other hummer away, it may be necessary to locate some of the feeders beyond his territory, or range of vision.

Keeping feeders clean and filled is an important part of a successful hummingbird feeding station.

In spite of their remarkable swiftness, hummingbirds sometimes fall victim to cats and small hawks. If cats are in the neighborhood, it is best to hang the feeders at least six feet from the ground. So that birds can quickly go to cover in case of danger, feeders should be near dense foliage of some kind. At the same time, hummers need an exposed perch from which to view their surroundings. This can be a utility wire, a bare twig, or even a perch on a feeder.

Sugar Vs. Honey

After years of controversy, it has generally been accepted that sugar, not honey, should be used in formulating the solution for use in feeders. Proponents of honey claimed that honey was more nutritious and therefore a better food than sugar, which provides energy but neither vitamins or minerals. Mr. Tucker, as already noted, found that honey was overly attractive to bees and therefore he switched to sugar.

In 1949, Dr. Augusto Ruschi, a noted Brazilian authority on hummingbirds, discovered that a honey solution could produce a fatal fungus disease in hummers. Symptoms included a swelling of the tongue. Dr. Ruschi's findings were corroborated by Jan Roger van Oosten of Seattle who discovered the same disease when he used honey in feeding captive hummingbirds. Furthermore, honey solutions spoil much more quickly than sugar-based mixtures. Nancy Newfield, a well-known authority on hummingbirds, conducted an experiment in which she sterilized two identical jars and filled one with a honey syrup and the other with a sugar syrup. Both jars were heat-sealed and placed side-by-side in the sun. The honey syrup became cloudy in less than 24 hours, whereas the sugar syrup remained clear for six days!

Formulating the Solution

Another debate that has taken place for years is the ratio of sugar to water to use in making the solution. Hummingbirds respond well to sweetness. The sweeter the solution, the better they seem to like it. But evidence obtained with captive birds has indicated that an overly rich sugar solution can lead to liver damage and possible dehydration in birds that drink it. Over the years a solution strength of one part sugar to four parts water has become accepted as the correct proportion to use—not too rich, but sweet enough to satisfy the cravings of these birds. This ratio closely approximates the sucrose content of most flower blossom nectars.

To prepare the solution, $1/4$ cup of granulated white sugar should be added for each cup of water. Pour this solution into a sauce pan and bring to a boil on a stove. A few minutes of boiling kills bacteria and mold spores and causes any chlorine or fluorine in the water to evaporate. This will help to slow the spoiling, or fermentation, process. After the solution has been allowed to cool, you are ready to fill your feeders. Extra solution can be stored in your refrigerator until needed.

Food Coloring?

Whether or not to add red food coloring to the solution is another frequently debated question. Those who favor red coloring consider it helpful in bringing birds to feeders. However, since nearly all commercial feeders are decorated with red plastic flowers or red is included in some other way this argument is moot. Red is simply an attention-getting color as far as hummers are concerned. They respond well to almost any color that shows up well against a dark background. If your feeder does not have brightly colored parts, tying a red ribbon to it may alert hummingbirds to your offering.

Some users of red food coloring say they use it so that they can more easily see feeder solution levels from a distance. A minute amount can be added for this purpose, but generally speaking it is safest not to use any coloring at all. Be satisfied with white sugar, and do not use any substitutes or additives. They are not needed and may prove harmful. Avoid fortified commercial solutions, artificial sweeteners, brown sugar, syrups, and, above all, honey!

The Dangers of Mold

Even with white sugar we risk harming birds if we let the solution stay in the feeder too long. This does not happen if there are enough birds present to drink up the contents of a feeder reservoir in a relatively short time. But if the contents haven't disappeared after three or four days in hot weather (above 65° F.), or a week in cool weather, mold will begin to form. Mold may be a health hazard to the birds. Normally a hummingbird won't drink at a feeder if the solution has become clouded. But even a few sips might prove harmful.

We can avoid this risk by taking the feeder in and emptying it before mold sets in. Rinse the feeder with hot water and add fresh solution. If, by chance, traces of a black mold have appeared anywhere in openings or inside the feeder, a thorough

scouring and rinsing is necessary. A small bottle or percolator brush with a flexible wire handle (or a pipe cleaner or an old toothbrush) will allow you to remove mold that has collected in crevices. Hard to remove mold spots may necessitate soaking your feeder in hot soapy water. Some people advocate using a minute amount of bleach to disinfect a feeder. In either case, make sure you rinse your feeder thoroughly before refilling.

Bees and ants are also fond of nectar and may invade a feeder if they can get to it.

Ants, Bees, Wasps

As if competition for sugar water wasn't already keen enough (other birds, bats, moths, and butterflies visit feeders), members of the insect order Hymenoptera, which includes bees, wasps, and flying ants, sometimes appear in such numbers that even the hummingbirds give up. Ants are the easiest to cope with. A heavy application of petroleum jelly (such as Vaseline) on approach routes will usually discourage them. Apply fresh coatings as needed.

The stinging Hymenoptera are harder to discourage and create problems for both humans and hummingbirds. Once again petroleum jelly—this time applied to surfaces around feeding ports—is called for, but is not always totally effective. Salad oil has also been recommended for use in the same manner, but it tends to become rancid and hard. For those who dare take the personal risk, a vacuum cleaner used on surfaces frequented by honey bees or other members of the group will quickly remove these insects. Where and how to empty the bag can be a problem! Unfortunately, the bee guards offered with commercial feeders are seldom effective. They make it harder for hummingbirds to feed and do not completely exclude bees, wasps, yellow jackets, and the like. Moving the feeder or feeders to a new location may help to solve the problem.

Not everyone who feeds hummingbirds has a problem with insects such as these. Often all one has to do is wait and the insects will leave of their own accord. Bees and related insects sometimes visit feeders only when their natural sources of nectar are in short supply. When their favorite flowers come into bloom, they leave.

Tougher Than We Think

It is important to realize that hummingbirds will not always suffer every time we make a mistake in how to feed them. They are resourceful birds that are able to cope with adverse conditions of many kinds. For example, the tiny ruby-throated hummingbird wins our admiration by twice yearly completing one of the longest flights known for a hummingbird. With a nesting range that extends as far north as central Alberta and a wintering range that extends as far south as Costa Rica, these birds accomplish flights that were once regarded as impossible for a bird its size. Rubythroats have an average weight of only about three grams, but by storing fat before they depart are able to endure astonishingly long journeys. Many rubythroats make a 600-mile flight across the Gulf of Mexico twice yearly—this in addition to the other distance they have traveled. The rufous hummingbird's long flights are also spectacular, with some individuals traveling all the way from Alaska to southern Mexico and returning again in the spring.

Hummingbirds show their resiliency in other ways as well. They may nest as high as 11,000 feet in the Rockies and are able to endure cold winters with a little help on our part. They are also relatively long-lived, living to ripe old ages of as much as 10 to 14 years in captivity and known ages of five or six years in the wild. One banded wild hummer was documented at 11 years old, but this is probably unusual.

What better way to show our appreciation for these colorful, adaptive birds than by planting flowers for them and feeding them with the help of bird feeders! We are rewarded in many ways. The early hummer returning in the spring, looking for a feeder at exactly the same spot where it was the previous year tells us that the birds remember instinctively, and that it is time to begin a new round of preparing solutions and putting out feeders. □

Chapter 3

FEEDER BIRDS AND WHAT TO FEED THEM

In this chapter we look at those birds most likely to visit our feeders and yards and what we can provide to attract them. The species are arranged here in the same taxonomic order used in most field guides. This will allow you to refer to your field guide for field marks and other important information about the birds you feed. Some groups of birds which may visit our feeders are not included here, such as hawks, owls, gulls, ducks, and so on, since they are not generally considered feeder birds. Please see the index at the back of the book for quick access to a particular species.

Black oil sunflower seed is one of the best foods we can offer to birds.

Gallinaceous Birds

Gallinaceous birds spend most of their lives on the ground and are closely related to our domestic fowl. The quail, pheasants, and grouse that belong to this group are often regarded as game whose purpose is to provide sport for hunters. But these ever-alert game birds are being seen more and more in parks, yards, and gardens. Arriving at bird feeders in coveys, sometimes numbering in the dozens, they feed hurriedly for a while and then depart as quickly as they came. Well adapted for traveling on foot, they troop in one behind the other. Only when surprised do they take flight with a whirr of wings, scattering in all directions.

There is no need to offer them sunflower seeds or other more expensive food. The game birds are content with corn (whole kernels or cracked), wheat, oats, milo, and millet. In drier regions they require a supply of fresh water. Many state game departments provide drinking outlets, known as "guzzlers," where the birds can always find water. In our yards they visit birdbaths primarily for drinking purposes, not for bathing. The gallinaceous birds keep their feathers "clean" and parasite-free by taking dust baths.

In addition to our native gallinaceous birds here in the West, we also have other species which have been introduced to provide sport. The ring-necked pheasant, found today in many areas across the continent, is the best-known of the introduced species. The first successful introduction of this pheasant from Asia was in Oregon in 1881. Partial to agricultural areas where few native game birds are present, the ring-necked has filled a void. It occurs in greatest numbers in the northern Great Plains, where another introduced game bird, the gray partridge, native to the Old World, has become established. A third introduced game bird, the chukar, also an Old World species, makes its home in barren mountainous regions where few native game birds could exist. Of the three species mentioned, only the ring-necked pheasant is a frequent visitor to bird feeders. During the spring, the male ring-necked, conspicuous in his gaudy plumage, may arrive with as many as six or seven hens, all of them members of his harem. During the winter, the two sexes of this species tend to stay apart.

Most of our native quail are found in the Southwest and northward into California, Utah, and Colorado. Jaunty-looking birds with prominent head plumes or crests, they readily enter our yards seeking food and are a pleasure to watch. The scaled quail is found from southern Texas to Colorado and Arizona. Scaled quail are very strong runners and will fly only as a last resort. At the campgrounds at Big Bend National Park, where many visitors set up feeding stations at their campsites, I observed these quail traveling in pairs about the grounds searching for food tidbits. The birds readily accepted the bread and scratch feed I scattered for them.

The arid Southwest from western Texas to southeastern California is the home of the Gambel's quail, a boldly marked bird with a tear-drop-shaped head plume that curves forward beyond the bill. This highly gregarious quail forms coveys sometimes numbering up to 200 birds, which can alarm people who feed them when so many converge upon the feeders at one time. Coveys numbering from 20 to 50 birds are more usual.

The more westward-ranging California quail has the same head plume and bears a strong resemblance to the Gambel's quail. The ranges of the two species meet in the arid interior of southern California. The California quail has been successfully introduced in other western states and in other parts of the world, even as far away as New Zealand! I wasn't surprised when I saw one within the shadow of the capitol dome in Salt Lake City, Utah. Parks, cemeteries, and campuses are as much a part of this bird's habitat as the desert scrublands.

The mountain quail, with a narrow, two-pronged head plume that curves backward instead of forward, is quite similar in appearance to the California and Gambel's. The mountain quail is found in the mountains of the Far West, where, in the fall and again in the spring, the birds perform a remarkable migration. They descend on foot from their high mountain range to lower elevations as winter approaches and return again on foot in the spring.

In southern parts of Arizona and New Mexico, and in western Texas, there is always a chance of seeing the Montezuma quail, with its bizarre facial pattern. Less of a grain-eater than other quail, this harlequinlike bird feeds chiefly on bulbs and tubers. But as many as four or five at a time will search the ground below bird feeders for milo and other grains.

The northern bobwhite can be expected at feeders in the Great Plains, to eastern Colorado and New Mexico, over most of Texas, and in isolated pockets in the Northwest, but it is largely a bird of the East.

Pigeons and Doves

To have a large flock of pigeons or doves descend upon the bird feeder is wonderful at first, but can become a nuisance. The food supply quickly vanishes as, with rapid pecking motions, the birds pick up food on the ground, meticulously searching the same area over and over. Then, dexterously teetering upon perches too small for them, they turn their attention to the hanging feeders. A spacious crop enables them to hold large quantities of food before it is passed along to the digestive system. This means that after a hearty meal they aren't likely to return for a time.

The terms "pigeon" and "dove" are used interchangeably, with larger species generally being called pigeons. In the West we have only one common pigeon—the band-tailed pigeon—which has both an inland population in the Rockies and a more coastal one from southern Alaska southward through California.

Band-tailed pigeons are handsome birds and are generally welcomed at feeders if they do not come in large numbers. Donald Clark of Bolinas, California plays host to about 30 bandtails the entire year. He likes them, saying they feed peacefully among themselves with little jostling and pushing. They are able to master nearly all of his feeders and, after a period of intense feeding, they leave the feeders to other birds.

The bandtail's natural diet consists of acorns and a wide variety of fruits and berries. At bird feeders, corn, wheat, sunflower seeds, and suet or suet mixes are equally popular. Like other pigeons and doves, bandtails drink long and copiously without raising their heads to swallow as seen in most other birds.

The mourning dove, found nearly everywhere from southern Canada southward, requires relatively open ground for its feeding purposes. It finds much of its food in cultivated fields and along roadsides. A complete "vegetarian," the mourning dove feeds upon weed seeds, seeds of grasses, and grain. As an aid to digestion, it eats large quantities of grit and seems to require small amounts of salt.

Graceful and swift of flight, and possessing one of the saddest of all bird songs, the mourning dove endears itself to most people. But its popularity decreases when too many come flocking to bird feeding stations. A feeder with a large flock of these doves present will find them forever quarreling among themselves, taking up space, and eating more than their share.

Since mourning doves do not leave as promptly as do band-tailed pigeons, even the smallest seeds are not overlooked. These birds will spend lengthy sessions picking up the small niger (thistle) seeds that fall to the ground from hanging feeders. All the other seeds and grain offered at bird feeders are also to their liking including buckwheat and rape, which are poorly received by other birds. In some ways it is helpful having mourning doves clean up after other birds, since their appetites ensure that food will not be left to spoil and create a possible health problem.

The other western doves have very much the same habits as the mourning dove. But the white-winged dove of southern Texas and the Southwest eats a far wider range of foods. This dove is nearly omnivorous and will accept almost anything offered at bird feeders, including banana, cheese, nut meats, and melon seeds. In the wild, seeds and grain are eaten along with many fruits and berries. A common bird in towns and cities, the whitewing nests in shade trees and in orange groves. After the nesting season, a large share of the population flies south to spend the winter in Mexico and Central America. The white-tipped dove is another very common feeder visitor in South Texas, its range just extending across the border from Mexico.

Both urban and ranch life have their attractions for a small dove with a pointed tail. This is the Inca dove, a bird with much the same range as the white-winged dove. To the delight and occasional dismay of those who are trying to supply birds with adequate amounts of seeds and grain, as many as 200 or more Incas will arrive for the day and spend their time milling around wherever food has been scattered. The birds also spend part of their time on overhead wires or wandering about on lawns, streets, and driveways. They seem to like to be where people are, probably because food is more easily found. Cracked corn, wheat, millet, and milo are among their favorite foods.

Common ground-doves, familiar birds in Florida and the Southeast, share some of the same range in the West with white-winged and Inca doves, but are not nearly as abundant as the last two. Like the Inca, the common ground-dove is small but has a short, rounded tail. Its food tastes and feeding habits are much the same as those of the Inca.

In addition to the species already mentioned, some bird feeders in the West can claim the ringed turtle-dove and the spotted dove. Both are introduced species that have become established in southern California.

Mourning doves and rock doves feed on the ground beneath a busy feeder.

The feral rock dove or pigeon is far more independent. Common in agricultural districts and very much in evidence in towns and cities, this is another Old World import which has been with us since Colonial days. Rock doves nest primarily on buildings and bridges in our cities and towns. While rock doves do not rely solely on humans for their food, a big part of their diet comes from us either directly or indirectly. Foods they will eat include most of the inexpensive seed types already mentioned, bread crumbs, table scraps, and so on.

Roadrunners

An extraordinary change in lifestyle has brought the greater roadrunner into ever closer contact with humans. Formerly this long-legged member of the cuckoo family was regarded as a bird of the great open space, but lured by food offerings and other easy food sources, the adaptable roadrunner has taken up residence in outlying suburbs. Here it sometimes accepts hamburger, hot dog pieces, and other meat scraps as a substitute for the snakes and lizards that make up a large share of its diet. Roadrunners can become a nuisance by pecking upon windows and glass doors, apparently asking for more. At a home in a California town, a pair of roadrunners which were used to being fed, nested in a flower bed outside a bedroom window!

Within its broad range from western Louisiana to California, roadrunners still roam wilder regions. But with the arrival of motor vehicles, they no longer, as they once did, appear to test their skills by trying to out run horsemen and horse-drawn carriages.

Woodpeckers

Regarded as forest dwellers, the woodpeckers offer a number of surprises to those of us who get to know them. Several species live in open country and come into yards whether or not trees are present. This is especially true of the Gila woodpecker, with a range extending from southeastern California to southwestern New Mexico. The Gila drills holes into the trunks of saguaro cactus and whatever other sites it can find for nesting purposes. It is an adaptable species that prospers either in the semi-desert, where it has always made its home, or in well-planted suburbs of cities such as Phoenix. As one of the most omnivorous of the woodpeckers, it eats fruits, berries, and insects in the wild and almost anything that is offered at bird feeders. M. French Gilman, whose experiments I referred to in

Chapter 1, listed meat, raw or cooked, watermelon, peaches, pears, and corn-on-the-cob as foods the Gila woodpecker readily accepted at his feeders. The Gilas were the most aggressive of his bird guests and were usually successful in keeping all the others away when they were eating. But on one occasion, a Bendire's thrasher that had been pinned down and severely pounded by a Gila woodpecker suddenly righted itself and "gave the woodpecker the thrashing of his career," Gilman reported.

Similar feeding habits are found in the gilded flicker, a race of the northern flicker that inhabits the same kind of country as the Gila woodpecker, also nesting in saguaro cactus. Like the Gila, it is quite fond of watermelon at feeding stations.

In Oklahoma and Texas, the closely related golden-fronted woodpecker takes the place of the Gila. It has much the same habitat and food preferences. It readily visits bird feeding stations where suet, bread, halved orange, or halved grapefruit are offered. I once observed one pounding at a discarded candy bar containing pieces of peanuts.

Taking the place of the East's red-headed woodpecker in the West is the Lewis' woodpecker, which is named for Captain Meriwether Lewis of the famed Lewis and Clark Expedition. This bird has the unwoodpeckerlike flight of a crow, flying in a straight line instead of the bouncy, undulating flight of other woodpeckers. It is found in open woodland and heavily cut-over tracts. About the same size as the red-headed, the Lewis' is equally fond of acorns, which it often stores for future consumption. In fall and winter, the Lewis' sometimes embarks upon massive flights southward that take it to the southern Great Plains and border regions of the Southwest.

At feeding stations, the Lewis' tends to become possessive, chasing all the other birds away. Judith Fishback, who feeds birds in Flagstaff, Arizona, calls the Lewis' "a bully, a dog in the manger that will not tolerate any other birds at or near the feeders." At a Colorado bird feeder, Lewis' woodpeckers ate cottage cheese, suet mixes, and soft apples. Other feeder foods taken include whole or cracked corn and mixed birdseed.

The aptly named acorn woodpecker of Oregon, California, and parts of the Southwest, is seldom found far from oak trees. Acorns make up approximately half of its food on an annual basis and as much as 100 percent when the supply is plentiful. If not eating acorns, the birds are busy storing them for future use. Each acorn is placed in a hole drilled just the right size to fit it. Cavities to hold acorns are excavated in the bark of trees, utility

*Lewis' wood-
peckers will
come to suet,
and will also
eat corn and
peanuts.*

poles, and even sides of wooden buildings. This species will visit feeding stations in great numbers only when its favorite acorns are in short supply. Unlike the Lewis' woodpecker, they feed peacefully among themselves and with other birds. Foods taken include suet, doughnuts, peanuts, cracked corn, and, best liked of all, sunflower seeds. Sugar water for hummingbirds is also readily consumed by acorn woodpeckers.

As the red-headed woodpecker expands its range limits westward across the Great Plains and into the Rockies, it can be expected to intrude upon territory held by acorn woodpeckers. These birds have similar tastes and will compete seriously with each other. If you live in an area where the ranges of red-headed and acorn woodpeckers overlap, be on the lookout for very interesting behavior, especially if males of both species try to claim your feeder territorially.

Both hairy and downy woodpeckers are present in wooded parts of the West, and, as everywhere, come readily to our feeders where suet or suet-mixes are offered. Much the same is true of Nuttall's woodpecker, a relative with a range largely restricted to California. The ladder-backed woodpecker is fairly common as a feeder visitor in many parts of the Southwest, though not nearly so regular, nor as omnivorous as the Gila. One or more of our species of sapsuckers, the Williamson's, red-breasted, red-naped, and yellow-bellied (in northwestern Canada) can be attracted to your feeding station. The sapsuckers are suet eaters and will accept halved apple and sugar water.

The northern flicker with a range that extends from coast to coast responds to a variety of foods. Suet, sunflower, halved orange, apple, and avocado are well received. I have seen flickers so engrossed in probing for ants in sidewalk crevices and lawns that they scarcely notice passers-by. Flickers also frequently forage on the ground. If you have an anthill in your yard, watch for a flicker to discover it.

Jays

Omnivorous applies as readily to the jays as it does to some of the woodpeckers. Jays are mostly non-migratory. Since they often face harsh winters they have learned to eat almost anything. If one source of food disappears, they go to another. Like a number of other birds that stay with us through the winter, jays store surplus food early in the season and come back later, after the harvest, to search for it. That some of this food is never retrieved is seen in the many oaks that sprout where jays have buried acorns, far from other oak trees. The same thing sometimes happens with sunflower seeds taken from the feeder.

Handsome plumages and clever ways win friends for the jays even though they are guilty at times of robbing the nests of other birds. These alert, noisy, and intelligent birds keep us amused and even add life in winter to otherwise dull surroundings. In the West we have seven jays, compared to only one, the blue jay, found throughout most of the East.

The gray jay of Canada and more northern states, is primarily a wilderness bird which does not always wait for us to feed it. By stealth or boldness, it takes whatever it can carry away. Those of us who have picnicked or camped in remote mountain areas know the gray jay well. Entering tents and cabins, often arriving as soon as smoke indicates the presence of food being cooked, the gray jay has a sharp eye for snatchable food, including bacon and other meats, baked beans, bread, cheese, and even non-edibles like soap. Whatever it doesn't eat right away, it stores for future use.

In recent years the gray jay has added ski lodges and slopes to the places it visits for food. At a ski resort in Colorado, I once observed that the gray jays congregated wherever people were eating their lunches out in the open. One man, in the process of lifting an egg sandwich to his mouth, had the entire sandwich snatched away from him by a gray jay that suddenly swooped in and disappeared almost before he knew what had happened. All day the jays were busily inspecting parked cars and keeping a close watch upon the skiers. One had the impression that they were enjoying the sport as much as the skiers themselves.

At Crater Lake National Park in Oregon, a group of gray jays were in the habit of visiting each car in a parking area until they found one with occupants who would feed them. Here and wherever else they come into competition with the larger, more formidable Clark's nutcracker, they hastily retreat. If there is anything a gray jay can't tolerate, it is competition with other birds for food. This is probably why they rarely appear at bird feeding stations. They are wilderness birds and seem content with "robbing" the occasional campsite, hence their colloquial name, "camp robber."

The larger, very handsome Steller's jay shares the western wilderness with the gray jay but is much more forward about visiting feeding stations. Indeed, in some parts of the West, the Steller's makes itself at home in towns and cities. Lording it over other birds, a Steller's jay will dominate our bird feeders for whatever time it needs to eat and carry away food to store for future use. Its food preferences at feeders include sunflower, peanuts, suet, and white bread.

Similar in habits and behavior to other jays is the scrub jay, formerly called California jay. Although present nearly everywhere in California, it has a range that extends from central Texas to the Pacific Coast and an eastern population restricted to Florida. Arthur C. Bent, in his *Life Histories of North American Birds*, says that the scrub jay is less shy, much bolder, more impertinent, and more mischievous than the blue jay. Bird feeders who attract scrub jays either like or dislike this high-spirited bird. They hold its nest robbing proclivities against it, but find compensation in its antics and friendly ways.

A friend of mine in Los Angeles used to carry peanuts with him to give the scrub jays when he went out for a walk, often leaving some in a paper bag on the lawn to let the jays help themselves. One day, to see what would happen, he closed the bag by twisting the top. Outraged, the jays spent part of the day in unsuccessful attempts to open the bag.

A scrub jay can carry away as many as a hundred sunflower seeds in five or six trips to the feeder. Some are held in the throat and others in the beak. If the jay is not hungry, all of them will be buried. Even food like bread, which easily spoils, is buried or hidden in crevices. Acorns as well as almonds and English walnuts, are high priority items on this jay's menu. Besides sunflower and peanuts, the jays readily accept doughnuts and other bread products.

In addition to the widespread species already mentioned, the West has two other jays with restricted ranges. One of them is the colorful green jay of southern Texas, and the other is the

gray-breasted jay of the southwestern mountains. Still another
jay makes its home in parts of the West. This is the blue jay so
familiar to Easterners and now spreading westward across the
northern Great Plains. The blue jay, which has been seen as far
west as Washington and Oregon, may become a familiar feeder
visitor as it is in the East in decades to come.

Jay Relatives:
Nutcrackers, Magpies, and Crows

Other members of the jay family, the nutcrackers, magpies,
and crows, have many traits in common with our jays, differing
mainly in appearance. The pinyon jay has the coloration of a jay
but in nearly all other respects is crowlike. Its blue plumage does
not disguise the fact that it has a short crowlike tail, it hops and
walks like a crow, and has the strong, direct flight of a crow. Jay
or crow, the pinyon is highly gregarious and embarks upon
massive flights during some years. Leaving the oak and pin-
yon-clad mountain slopes and foothills, pinyon jays wander far
and wide when their natural foods are in short supply. During
the fall of 1961, tens of thousands of the birds were said to have
passed through Silver City in southwestern New Mexico.

Feeding stations are patronized both within the bird's home
range and during periods of nomadic wandering. They add col-
or to our feeding stations as they feed peacefully among themselves and with other birds. Only when they arrive in large
flocks are they unwelcome, as the sheer weight of their numbers
keeps every other bird away. The "blue crow," as it is sometimes
called, has tastes that run to nut meats, suet, meat scraps, and
sunflower seeds.

Another bird with an uncertain taxonomic status is the
Clark's nutcracker. This species can be described as a crowlike
jay, attired in gray and black, possessing the powerful bill and
flight of a woodpecker. Its behavior when it comes to people and
food, however, is distinctly jaylike. It shares the high mountains
of the West with gray and Steller's jays. Like these two, it will
boldly enter tents and cabins in search of food and often keeps
a close watch upon campgrounds and picnic areas.

At Crater Lake National Park in southwest Oregon, the
Clark's nutcracker, along with gray and Steller's jays, is a major
tourist attraction. People enjoy feeding a bird that will come to
their hand to accept food or that will catch peanuts in midair.
The Clark's nutcrackers readily oblige but prefer to keep the
show to themselves. Gray jays and Steller's leave discreetly

*One visit
from a crow
can put a big
dent in the suet
supply.*

when the nutcrackers are entertaining visitors, knowing they cannot compete with these larger, more aggressive birds.

If food is scarce in the mountains where the nutcrackers make their home, they band together, like the pinyon jay, and seek richer supplies at lower elevations. During some years they invade towns and cities and even reach the Pacific Coast. They will visit bird feeders but not in overwhelming numbers. When they do appear, they favor meat scraps, suet, bread, and other bakery products. Their fondness for meat has earned them the name "meat bird."

Crows, magpies, and ravens are normally too distrustful of humans to become regular patrons at feeding stations. This is probably just as well since many people have all they can handle playing host to other members of the jay family. A little less reluctant than the crows and ravens, magpies will sometimes become steady visitors at suet feeders maintained by ranchers. The black-billed magpie has a wide range that extends from central Alaska to the Rockies and central Great Plains, while its close relative, the yellow-billed magpie, is found only in the central valleys of California and nearby hill country.

Natalie Owens, who lives in ranching country in northern New Mexico, is perhaps one of the few people who can say that she has bird feeders that are well-attended by pinyon jays, black-billed magpies, crows, and ravens. She states that "the birds appear to eat absolutely anything and lots of it, including dog food pellets!" Other birds visiting her feeders include yellow-headed and red-winged blackbirds, mourning doves, scrub jays, and Lewis' woodpeckers. An unusual assemblage for any feeding station!

Titmice and Chickadees

Birds in the family known as the titmice, which includes the chickadees, are favorites at bird feeders and are among the easiest of birds to attract to our feeders. Inquisitive and interested in everything taking place in the yard, they are apt to be the first birds to appear at new feeders or newly activated ones. Other birds watch them closely and travel along with them in loose flocks, probably because they know that the active, sharp-eyed titmice will lead them to sources of food. This explains why small woodpeckers, nuthatches, and kinglets so often arrive at bird feeders at about the same time as the titmice.

The titmice show a preference for sunflower seed, suet, suet mixes, doughnuts, and mixed birdseed. Close ties to the jay family are seen in the way they fly off with food and pound it apart with their bills. Like the jays, they store food for future use. Their ability to find food under difficult circumstances permits the titmice to endure cold northern winters and short daylight hours.

The most conspicuous difference between titmice and chickadees is that titmice have crests. In terms of behavior, chickadees tend to be somewhat more inquisitive and are more easily persuaded to take food from our hand.

In the West, we have a richness of these small, friendly birds. Besides the black-capped chickadee, which is found from coast to coast, the West has the chestnut-backed chickadee with a range extending from Alaska to southern California; a mountain species, the mountain chickadee; and a far northern species, the boreal chickadee, which has a range extending from central Alaska across Canada to the Atlantic Coast.

Two closely related titmouse species are the plain titmouse and the tufted titmouse. The tufted titmouse's range includes most of Texas and the eastern Great Plains. The plain titmouse is found from extreme western Texas, north to Wyoming and west to California and Oregon. Like the chickadees, the plain titmouse is a common visitor to bird feeders.

Less well-known and with a much smaller range in this country is the bridled titmouse, which lives in the mountainous districts of central and southern Arizona and southwestern New Mexico. Its checkered facial pattern gives it a distinctive look that is almost clownlike. This titmouse is regularly seen at the few bird feeders within its habitat. It is more commonly attracted to scraps at picnic areas.

Although in different families, the verdin and bushtit resemble the titmice in behavior and habits enough to be discussed along with them. The very active, noisy little verdin of southwestern desert country is an altogether different looking bird than the titmouse. In the adult, the plumage is largely grayish except for a yellow head. A resident of semi-desert, dotted with mesquite and thorny shrubs, the verdin would appear to be very much out of place in residential areas of towns and cities. But like the Inca dove, cactus wren, and the desert thrashers, it has been lured to cities such as Tucson and Phoenix by the presence of plantings, water, and food at bird feeders. The verdin visits hummingbird feeders and is also attracted to suet and suet mixes. Those who furnish the fruit of the pomegranate at their feeders may be rewarded by visits from these busy little birds.

The four-and-a-half-inch-long bushtit is as small as the verdin, and, like the verdin, has found its way into towns and cities, though it prefers oak woodlands to the desert habitat preferred by the verdin. Traveling about in large flocks, the tiny bushtits seem to appear from nowhere, inspecting the foliage for minute insects. They feed busily for a while and then are gone. The same sequence of events takes place at bird feeders where the attraction is suet, suet mixes, doughnuts, and peanut butter. Few people who live in the bushtit's wide range through the West succeed in attracting them, and those that do must watch closely to catch a glimpse of this flighty bird.

Nuthatches

Like the titmice, nuthatches are favorites of those who feed birds. The red-breasted nuthatch, with nearly a continentwide distribution, can be expected almost anywhere in wooded parts of the West. It is present as a resident in more northern sections and a winter visitor in the south. The white-breasted nuthatch, with an equally wide range, is a permanent resident of wooded regions. Found from south-central British Columbia southward, the pygmy nuthatch has a patchy distribution in mountainous country all the way into Mexico. It is largely a bird of the ponderosa pine forest.

The white-breasted nuthatch is the largest of the three and is very possessive in defending its sources of food. Seldom are more than one or two seen at a bird feeder. The red-breasted and pygmy nuthatches are somewhat smaller and less aggressive. On the other hand, the highly gregarious pygmy nuthatch may arrive in sizable flocks and inundate the feeders.

*Pygmy nuthatches
wedge sunflower
seeds into a bark
crevice and pound
them open.*

Titmice and nuthatches habitually fly off with one or more seeds in their bills. If they have a sunflower seed or shelled nut,

they will place it in a suitable crevice, often in the bark of a tree, and pound it open using their bill as a chisel, hence the name "nuthatch." Much of the food these birds take at feeders is carefully tucked away for future use.

Besides sunflower seed and nut meats, the nuthatches respond readily to suet, suet mixes, cracked corn, melon seeds, and bread. In the wild, acorns and pine seeds make up a large share of the diet of the white-breasted nuthatch; red-breasted and pygmy nuthatches feed largely on pinecone seeds. All three also consume many insects.

Creepers

Creepers are small, brownish birds, with a wide breeding range that extends from Alaska southward through the mountains and eastward to the Atlantic Coast. They can be expected almost anywhere in wooded areas in winter. Creepers are tree-trunk foragers (they "creep" up tree trunks) whose brown plumage matches the bark. They are primarily solitary birds and are easily overlooked, though they sometimes associate with winter feeding flocks of titmice and chickadees. If no other birds are present, a brown creeper will almost surreptitiously approach a feeder and sample the suet or suet mix. Now and then a creeper will drop to the ground to search for fallen tidbits or insects.

Wrens

Our wrens are inquisitive birds, forever searching for small prey in nooks and crannies of brush piles, and even in and about human habitations. With their scolding notes, they are noisy birds that only now and then pay a visit to our bird feeder. This is not so true of the cactus wren found from southern Texas to southern California. This largest of the wrens can be easily mistaken for a small thrasher. The cactus wren is equally at home in desert scrublands or well-planted suburbs, and is omnivorous in its feeding habits. Foods accepted at feeders include suet, peanut butter, nut meats, bread, watermelon, and halved apple. The Bewick's wren, common in warmer parts of the West, will stop by at a feeder long enough to sample nut meats, bread, or cookie crumbs. Similar tastes are seen in the house wren, the most widespread of our North American wrens. Even the tiny winter wren, possessor of one of the most melodious of all bird songs, will pay an occasional visit to a bird feeder.

Mockingbirds and Thrashers

Mimic thrushes, as they are called—the mockingbirds and thrashers—have remarkable vocal skills and are generally popular with those who feed birds. But the northern mockingbird loses some of its popularity when overly aggressive individuals begin chasing other birds away from feeders and berry-bearing shrubs. Fortunately, this is usually a temporary activity engaged in by territorial first-winter males. With the exception of seeds and grain, most feeding station foods appeal to the mockingbird. Mockingbirds are somehow not inclined to take food at bird feeders, seeming to prefer receiving it directly from us at windowsills or doorsteps. If food is not promptly forthcoming, some mockers have been known to show their displeasure by tapping upon window panes or scolding just outside the room we are in. Almost any soft food—bakery products, steamed raisins, sliced apple or orange—is to their liking. Formerly, the mockingbird was considered a bird of the more southern parts of the country, but in recent years it has been moving steadily northward. On the West Coast it has reached Oregon and Washington.

Arriving from a different direction, the mockingbird's two close cousins, the gray catbird and brown thrasher, have been moving westward across the Great Plains. They, too, are occasional visitors to bird feeders. The gray catbird has food preferences similar to the mockingbird, whereas the brown thrasher is more omnivorous.

In contrast to the East, with its single brown thrasher, the West has seven species, eight counting the brown thrasher. Each differs somewhat in size and coloration with bill length and overall shape being helpful clues to their identification. The long-billed thrasher of southern Texas, curve-billed, crissal, and Le Conte's thrashers of the Southwest, and California thrasher have long, decurved bills. Relatively short bills are found in the sage thrasher of middle portions of the Rocky Mountain region and Bendire's thrasher of the Southwest.

Response to feeding stations varies considerably among the seven thrasher species. Those responding quite well include the long-billed, curve-billed, and California thrashers. Although primarily desert dwellers, crissal and Bendire's thrashers will visit feeders wherever they come into contact with civilization. Still largely aloof from human-made habitat, Le Conte's and sage thrashers rarely make an appearance. No matter the species, all seem to have a special liking for sliced watermelon. Other foods to try on thrashers include cracked corn, milo, millet, suet, and bread.

The California thrasher is very much in evidence at bird feeders, and like the others, is a ground feeder that uses its bill expertly to break open or uncover food. Almost all of the foods we offer are well-received, whether they are delicacies like steamed raisins, figs, or pomegranate, or the standard sunflower or mixed birdseeds, cracked corn, suet, and bakery products. This thrasher can be expected at bird feeders in California from about San Francisco southward. No more than one pair is likely to be in residence in any one yard, or at one feeding station.

Robins are habitual bathers, easily attracted to a clean birdbath.

Thrushes and Close Relatives

The best-known member of the thrush family is the American robin, a bird found nearly everywhere and a familiar sight as it hops about on lawns looking for worms. When fall comes, robins turn increasingly to fruits and berries as their prime sources of food. Although a few robins winter as far north as southern British Columbia, thousands head south, stripping trees and shrubs of their fruit along the way. Only a relatively small number are detained by food at bird feeders. But occasionally a robin will take up winter residence in a yard and attempt to defend its sources of food from other birds.

At the feeder, the robin prefers soft foods such as suet, currants, raisins, cornbread, doughnuts, white bread, nut meats, and halved apple. Robins spend an inordinate amount of time drinking and bathing. Dozens will gather around a birdbath and quickly empty it. Their insatiable thirst is triggered by the herbaceous part of their diets, something also seen in other fruit-eaters.

The robin's close relative, the varied thrush, leaves its home in the North in large numbers during some years and appears at lower elevations all the way to Southern California. Cold, snow, and food shortage are all factors causing these incursions. Once they have reached the lowlands, flocks of varied thrushes join robins in visiting orchards and trees, such as the mountain ash. Both species prefer partly rotten apples over fresh ones. As a rule, only when the natural food supply begins to be exhausted do varied thrushes begin to visit feeding stations. Here they tend to be irritable, quarrelsome guests, fighting among themselves and chasing other birds away. Nevertheless, varied thrushes are such colorful birds that most people are pleased to have them in their yards and at their bird feeders. Apples are as popular with the birds at feeders as they are in the wild. Bread, suet mixes, millet, and kitchen scraps are also readily eaten.

The Townsend's solitaire is another bird that breeds in the Far North and in the mountains. Similar seasonal factors bring solitaires to the lowlands, but never in sizable flocks. As its name indicates, the Townsend's is a loner. A single bird perched on the highest spire of an evergreen, surveying the scene around it is often our first view of this wilderness species. When solitaires do appear in residential districts, they show much more interest in fruits and berries on ornamental plantings than anything at the bird feeder. It is a treat to see one of these slender gray birds feeding at the suet or eating sunflower seeds, mixed birdseeds, or softened raisins.

Of the brown-backed thrushes with speckled breasts, only the hermit thrush is a likely feeding station visitor. We will recognize this northern and mountain species by its contrasting reddish tail, which it slowly raises and lowers. In winter, the hermit thrush is found all the way from the more southern portions of its breeding range to Central America. Small seeds and grain and sliced apple are some of the feeding station foods that appeal to this uncommon visitor.

The wrentit is a retiring, streaked brown bird with a long tail; it is found in coastal scrublands from southern Oregon southward through California. It is a puzzling, small bird that was once placed in a family of its own. It seems out of place with the thrushes. In terms of behavior it is wrenlike, keeping to dense shrubs and revealing its presence by a loud ringing song.

In the same way as the wrens, a wrentit will come into the open only long enough to examine curiously the bird feeders and their contents. Before returning to cover it may sample the suet, peanut butter, chick feed, or bread. Taking first priority wherever available, though, is sugar water at hummingbird feeders.

Bluebirds

It is always a treat to see bluebirds. After the breeding season, bluebirds sometimes appear in large flocks that range throughout the plains and lowlands. The western bluebird, which breeds from British Columbia southward, can be recognized by its contrasting blue and chestnut plumage. It is attracted to yards and gardens by the presence of water and by fruit and berry-bearing plants. Only belatedly does it seem to find its way to bird feeders. Here it eats suet, suet mixes, small seeds, and bread crumbs. Some adventurous feeder operators have lured bluebirds to their feeders with live mealworms, purchased from local fishing supply or bait stores.

The mountain bluebird has a wider range, breeding all the way from Alaska southward. The male is a solid sky blue and the female a somewhat pale gray with traces of blue. More partial to open country than the western bluebird, the mountain bluebird is not usually seen around human habitations and is much less expected at bird feeders. The eastern bluebird is widespread in the southern Great Plains, and in Texas, and even has a local population in Southeastern Arizona. Water is more of an attraction than food and may even attract numerous individuals. Many people who feed birds find that when they provide housing for bluebirds nearby, they often have more luck attracting them to their feeders as well.

Kinglets

Although fall migration sees most ruby-crowned and golden-crowned kinglets traveling to warmer regions, a few remain as far north as southwestern Canada. Along with chickadees, kinglets roam the woodlands searching for minute forms of insect life. Those that show up at feeding stations are probably following the example of the chickadees with which they tag along. The ruby-crowned kinglet rather than the golden-crowned is the more likely of the two to visit our feeding stations, attracted by suet, doughnuts, and cornbread.

Waxwings

Dapper, well-groomed birds, the waxwings not only have an air of elegance about them but they have the manners that go with it. They do not quarrel among themselves or with other birds when eating. In fact, waxwings even have a "polite" way of passing along a berry from bill to bill when lined up on the branch of a tree, a behavior which seems to be related to courtship. During the fall and winter, flocks of waxwings wander far and wide in search of food. After stripping a Russian olive or pyracantha of its fruit, they are off to feed upon similar fruits elsewhere.

Cedar waxwings are the continent's greatest wanderers. Leaving their wide breeding range (from southeastern Alaska through Canada and the northern states) in the fall, they begin to move southward. Some have even reached northern South America.

Bohemian waxwings, larger than the cedar, and which breed in Alaska and western Canada, perform similar but shorter

flights. After leaving their breeding grounds, they disperse in several directions—some traveling eastward as far as coastal Canada with the largest number following the Rockies southward. Some years, huge flocks of this waxwing wander throughout and beyond the species' normal range. During the winter of 1916-17 ornithological records show that there was a record invasion, with thousands appearing in Denver, Seattle, and other cities. Residents in Denver, fearing the birds would starve, began offering them food. Raisins were eagerly received by the birds, but canned peas were the choicest food of all!

People are always impressed by the complete fearlessness of these birds. They practically allow themselves to be picked up! After gorging on fruits and berries, the waxwings go into a comatoselike state. But after letting their digestive processes work for a while, they are soon recovered, once more eating as much as they can hold. Only a few of the foods offered at feeding stations appeal to either of the two waxwings. Raisins, currants, and sliced apple are the best three to try on the birds. As with the robin, waxwings also seem to need more water than other birds.

Warblers

Our warblers are brightly colored, small songbirds that impress us in much the same way as do the hummingbirds. Though we call them "our" warblers, they are essentially birds of the tropics that come north only to breed. If we see them at all, it is largely during spring and fall migration when the birds are going to and returning from northern nesting grounds. A few, including the common yellowthroat and yellow warbler, nest throughout much of North America.

As with hummingbirds, the migratory urge is not always

strong enough to see a complete exodus of all of the warblers in late summer and fall. Some drop out along the way and others have become established as residents or partial migrants, especially if there are reliable sources of food and water nearby.

The yellow-rumped warbler (formerly known as the Audubon's warbler in the West) is the best example of a warbler that may or may not undertake the expected return to the tropics. In winter, this abundant species can be found all the way from British Columbia to Panama. It is the warbler to expect at bird feeders in winter. Having a wide range of tastes, the yellow-rumped will accept suet, suet mixes, finely cracked corn, doughnuts, sliced apple, steamed raisins, and a variety of similar foods. Sugar water at hummingbird feeders is a popular food for warblers, too, especially the yellow-rumped.

Almost any North American warbler is a possibility at western bird feeders in winter. Every fall, a few strays from the East reach the Rockies and beyond to the Pacific Coast. Chances of seeing one at a feeding station are unpredictable. Much better luck can be had with typical western warblers that haven't departed for the tropics. Besides the yellow-rumped, warbler species to look for include the black-throated gray, common yellowthroat, hermit, Wilson's, orange-crowned, and Townsend's. The last two, along with the yellow-rumped, regularly spend the winter from southwestern British Columbia southward. Suet, suet mixes with peanut butter in them, finely chopped nut meats, doughnuts, cornbread, and sliced fruits are all good foods to use in luring warblers. Water, especially water in motion, is the best attractant of all.

In a class by itself is the painted redstart of Arizona and New Mexico. During summer in the mountain country where it breeds, this gaudy black, white, and red warbler is a casual visitor at hummingbird feeders in the Southwest. It is one of bird feeding's most thrilling sights to see this warbler at a feeder along with the hummingbirds!

Tanagers

Like so many of the hummingbirds and warblers, the tanagers are tropical birds that fly north for the one purpose of nesting and raising families. Male tanagers, especially, are brightly colored birds that everyone likes to see. Adult females and immature birds may be confusing to identify. When in doubt, consult your field guide. (Note: Elevation may be a clue to which tanager you are seeing. Summer tanagers nest in lowland areas of the Southwest, hepatic tanagers nest also in the Southwest, at elevations from 5,000 to 7,500 feet, and western tanagers nest throughout the West at higher elevations, above 7,500 feet.)

Being insect eaters, tanagers are not particularly receptive to feeding station foods. During the summer they may bring young to our feeders to sample fruit, a few seeds, or sugar water. Most often they begin showing an interest in feeder foods in fall and winter. The species most often seen at feeders at this time of the year is the summer tanager. The adult male, fortunately, retains its red plumage and therefore is easy to recognize. Southern California has the most winter feeder records for this species and there are a few others for other parts of the Southwest.

Tanagers prefer softer foods over seeds and grain. Among those that they accept at feeding stations are suet, doughnuts, bread, cornbread, apple, orange, and grapes. They will also visit birdbaths for drinking and bathing.

Cardinals, Grosbeaks, and Buntings

Thanks to the presence of the northern cardinal in parts of the West and pyrrhuloxia in the Southwest, the West can be said to have two cardinals. Both have large conical bills, prominent crests, and in the males, bright red coloration. As irrigated lands and green yards and gardens supplanted the desert habitat of the pyrrhuloxia and the somewhat less arid country of the cardinal, the two began to move into human-made habitat. Now both visit bird feeders in residential areas in the Southwest. In areas where both species occur, they eat peacefully together, usually feeding on the ground. They have similar tastes: sunflower seeds, cracked corn, milo, millet, and halved apple. The pyrrhuloxia has a liking also for halved tomato.

The black-headed and rose-breasted grosbeaks offer another example of two close relatives sharing parts of the same range. This occurs where the rose-breasted grosbeak, a bird primarily found in the East, and the black-headed grosbeak, representing the West, meet on the Great Plains. These two species are closely related and sometimes interbreed. Not entirely eastern, the rose-breasted grosbeak breeds as far west as British Columbia, Alberta, and Saskatchewan. Leaving the breeding ranges in the fall, members of these two species fly south to spend the winter in the tropics. Some drop out along the way and turn up at feeding stations. Southern California is one region likely to have wintering rose-breasted grosbeaks in very small numbers.

Chances of having either of the two grosbeaks at bird feeders

are highest during the summer breeding season. Seemingly tame
and confiding, they freely come into yards near wherever they
are nesting. The black-headed grosbeak is in the habit of visiting
campgrounds and picnic areas in the mountains in search of
food. At Zion National Park in Utah, the black-headeds are regarded as panhandlers. It is easy enough to provide for the
grosbeaks, since both respond readily to sunflower seed (a preferred food), suet, cracked corn, millet, bread, softened raisins,
halved apple, and halved orange.

The indigo bunting of the East is replaced in the Great Plains
region by the very similar lazuli bunting of the West. Both
buntings spend the winter in the tropics and have very similar
habits. The males of the two species are among the brightest and
most vividly colored of the small seed-eating birds. The iridescent, deep dark blue of the indigo male covers his entire body.
And, as if to outdo its eastern cousin, instead of an entirely blue
plumage, the male lazuli has a cinnamon band across the breast.
No wonder we love to see this bunting when it returns in
spring!

The lazuli bunting breeds from southern British Columbia
southward. It is not too particular about the habitats in which it
breeds; included are humid coastal regions, sagebrush, semi-
desert, and forested mountain slopes. Indeed lazulis are found
breeding anywhere from sea level to altitudes as high as 10,000
feet! One of the few habitats that it avoids during the nesting
season is the residential district. This helps explain why few are
seen at our bird feeders in summer. The spring and fall migration periods offer better opportunities to see these colorful birds
at feeders. Often traveling in flocks with sparrows and juncos,
the buntings drop by at feeders to sample millet, canary seeds,
and similar foods. Only rarely do they stay behind in winter.

Parts of the Southwest are in the range of the beautiful
painted bunting, which a few lucky feeder operators have man-
aged to attract. Along the Rio Grande, two Mexican buntings—
the varied bunting and blue bunting—occur in small numbers at
feeding stations in border areas in Texas, New Mexico, and Arizona during summer. However, the bunting most likely to visit
our feeding station is the colorful lazuli bunting.

It would be hard to find a bird whose range more closely
approximates the country's heartland than the dickcissel. Not
clearly eastern or western, the dickcissel includes the Midwest
and the eastern parts of the Great Plains in its range. Dickcissels
are sparrowlike birds that gather in large flocks in the fall, before

the bulk of the population retires to Mexico and northern South America for the winter. Invariably, sizable numbers go in opposite directions—some go west to the edge of the Rockies and others as far east as the Atlantic Coast.

Dickcissels that stay behind in winter are likely candidates to show up at our bird feeders. Often it will be a single bird that makes an appearance, mixed in with a flock of house sparrows. The two species are the same size and look and behave surprisingly alike. Dickcissels respond well to sunflower seed, wheat, millet, and milo.

Towhees, Sparrows, and Juncos

Vigorous scratchers, the towhees use their feet to rake away leaves with a characteristic two hops forward and a long sweep backward. Even though food is in plain sight at bird feeders, they continue to employ this energetic method. Of the five towhee species we have in the West, the brown towhee of the Pacific region and Southwest are by far the tamest and easiest to see. Within the brown towhee's range, nearly every yard with a feeder has at least one pair of these birds. They show themselves boldly on lawns, in driveways, picnic areas, and campgrounds. Brown towhees are as watchful as jays for any scraps we may leave behind, and are quick to claim anything edible.

Scarcely straying from the city block or ranchyard where it lives, the brown towhee seems to manage very nicely on a diet consisting of seeds, grain, a few insects, and whatever extra it can obtain from us. At feeders, the birds seem to prefer sunflower, cracked corn, oats, millet, and bread.

For those who want to keep abreast of the latest changes in nomenclature, it has recently been determined that there are two brown towhee species, not just one. A Pacific Coast form is now a full species, called the California towhee. In a separate range extending from Arizona to Oklahoma, southern Texas and southward into Mexico, an interior form—called the canyon towhee—is now the second of the two species. Without having to learn the minor differences between the two, since both birds are permanent residents it is safe to assume that any brown towhee in the Pacific Coast region is the California towhee and anywhere inland and eastward is the canyon towhee.

The Abert's towhee of Arizona and portions of bordering Southwestern states could be called a desert version of the brown towhee. It mainly differs from its close relatives by having a black patch on its face and throat. Although described by early writers as shy and nervous, this does not seem to be the case anymore. In our yards and at our bird feeders, it is almost as fearless as the brown towhee. The Abert's has moved into residential areas of Phoenix and other Arizona cities. Like the pyrrhuloxia, it seems to find human-made habitat as suitable a place to live as the desert. The food preferences of this towhee, like those of the two brown towhees, include small seeds and grain.

A towhee that breeds in the mountains at altitudes up to 11,000 feet is the green-tailed towhee. It is a sparrow-sized bird with a greenish back and tail, a white throat, and gray underparts tinged with green. Wherever it is feeding, it gives its presence away by a catlike mewing sound and noise of scratching in leaves. It sometimes appears at feeding stations during the breeding season, but more often during spring and fall migration when it occurs at lower elevations. A friendly bird, it will come to the doorsteps to receive bread crumbs and other scraps. At feeding stations it scratches as much as ever and aggressively holds its own against all other birds. Food preferences are similar to those of other towhees, and include berries, seeds, and insects. A few remain for the winter in southern Arizona, New Mexico, and Texas.

Green-tailed towhees will readily visit feeders for bread crumbs and small seeds.

The best known of the towhees is the rufous-sided towhee, which has a continentwide distribution. Rufous-sideds breed from Canada, south into Mexico and are present in the West in winter as far north as Colorado, Utah, and southern British Columbia. The western form of this towhee has white spots and markings on the wings and back and is sometimes called the spotted towhee. White spots on mostly black plumage, rufous sides, and white below make the male rufous-sided towhee a handsome bird and one that is easy to recognize.

In habits and behavior this towhee is very much the same wherever it is found. It is much more of a skulker than the other towhees, spending most of its time in dense undergrowth. Although a frequent patron at bird feeders, it seldom remains long and is easily frightened by other birds or any kind of disturbance. A typical feeder scene might see the male rufous-sided coming to a raised shelf where he feeds, nervously twitching his tail, while the female keeps to the ground busily scratching for fallen grain.

The rufous-sided towhees that remain in the north for the winter are very much at the mercy of the weather. When the ground is covered by ice or snow, the birds can no longer obtain their usual sources of food—seeds, fruits, and dormant insects.

Mortality can be high under these circumstances. Feeding stations often come to the rescue during such times. Here the towhees accept suet, suet mixtures, sunflower, millet, cracked corn, nut meats, and bread.

Sparrows

Not to be confused with the "imported" house sparrow, our native sparrows belong to a New World subfamily that also includes the towhees and juncos. Sparrows are mostly brownish, streaked, small birds that feed on the ground and travel in flocks. They also can pose a problem when it comes to identification. Of the 28 sparrow species that have breeding ranges partially or wholly in the West, fewer than half are birds that we can easily recognize and get to know at our feeding stations. The others are too shy to appear, or have different habitat and food preferences, and many are very difficult to recognize. A good example is the olive sparrow of South Texas. This drab Mexican species is a common feeder visitor in the arid scrublands of South Texas.

Although the rufous-crowned sparrow is as nondescript looking as any of the others, it deserves notice as one of the sparrows most likely to appear at feeding stations from Oklahoma and Texas to Arizona, and again from central California southward where a separate population exists. A black whisker mark helps separate this sparrow from the very similar field and chipping sparrows. The rufous-crowned is a frequent visitor to bird feeders and is receptive to being fed at mountain campgrounds and picnic areas. Because the rufous-crowned is present all year it can become a regular visitor, often appearing quite tame. Bread crumbs, millet, and other small seeds are to its liking.

Grouping the other sparrows likely to visit our feeding stations may help us in identifying them. Sparrows of the genus *Spizella* are small sparrows with clear breasts, streaked or reddish caps, and white wing bars. This group includes the American tree sparrow, chipping, clay-colored, Brewer's, and field sparrows. While these sparrows are found in different parts of western North America, all travel southward in the fall. During the nesting season when insects and other natural foods are plentiful these sparrows are unlikely to visit our feeders. But during fall migration with the coming of cold weather, whole flocks—sometimes including more than one species—appear in yards and at bird feeders. Preferring food scattered on the ground, sparrows in this group are content with finely cracked corn, millet, and canary seed.

The vesper and lark sparrows are open country birds which also travel south in the fall. In appearance, white outer tail feathers are a distinguishing feature in both. Both are unlikely feeder visitors, though each may take advantage of food and water during migration if it is readily available.

In the Southwest a distinctive, handsome sparrow once called the desert sparrow, makes its home in sagebrush and creosote bush country. Now called the black-throated sparrow, it sometimes appears in winter at bird feeders from southern California to western Texas. Its tastes run to millet, chickfeed, and bread. At one feeder in Tucson black-throated sparrows were attracted with the seeds of the barrel cactus.

Another sagebrush sparrow of the West is the aptly named sage sparrow with a range extending from southeastern Washington southward. It looks somewhat like the black-throated sparrow but is much less likely to visit bird feeders.

The lark bunting is another sparrow of the uncultivated open range. Not only is it not a bunting, to further confuse matters the male in breeding plumage most closely resembles a male bobolink. Solid black except for a large white patch on each wing, the male lark bunting is a beautiful bird indeed. Lark buntings travel south in large flocks during the fall but stay primarily on the open plains where they rarely find our bird feeders.

Identification problems pop up again when we try to separate Savannah, fox, song, Lincoln's, and swamp sparrows from each other. All have streaked breasts, brownish, streaked backs, and few helpful markings. Furthermore, forms or subspecies belonging to the same species occur and can look quite different in appearance. West Coast fox sparrows, for example, are dark, dusky brown birds—very different from the reddish-brown fox

In fall and winter look for mixed flocks of sparrows feeding on the ground around feeders.

sparrows of the East. Also song sparrows differ in color depending upon the habitats they occupy. Desert forms are very pale whereas song sparrows of the humid Pacific Northwest are so dark that in poor light they look almost black.

Fortunately sparrows can be studied at close range when they appear regularly at our feeding stations, giving us ample opportunity to note every detail of their their markings. Once we note the field marks of a sparrow species we can consult our field guide for an answer to its identity. Of the species mentioned, the fox and song sparrows are the most likely of all to find their way to feeding stations. Both have a habit of emerging from dense foliage, eating a while around the feeder and returning to cover again. Besides a liking for almost any seed and grain mixture, these two sparrows are also fond of nut meats, bread, and doughnuts. Scratching vigorously wherever food is available on the ground, these two help clean up after other birds have had their fill. Song sparrows are avid bathers and make frequent trips to the birdbath throughout the day.

A final group, called the crowned sparrows because of their bold head markings, includes the most distinctive sparrows of all: Harris', white-crowned, golden-crowned, and white-throated sparrows. Their appearance in the fall tells us that another phase in our bird feeding program is about to begin. Once established at a location where food is offered, the crowned sparrows are not likely to leave until spring migration gets underway. In parts of the West where they nest, white-crowned sparrows are often year-round visitors at bird feeders.

The Harris' sparrow, a mid-continent species, nests in the far north and most of the population spends the winter in a restricted range just 300 miles long and 100 miles wide from southern Kansas to south-central Texas. As if this winter range were too small, every fall some Harris' sparrows head either in an easterly or a westerly direction. Some do not stop until they reach the ocean, others drop out along the way. As already noted, this is the same kind of dispersal seen in the dickcissel. Wherever they spend the winter, Harris' sparrows take readily to feeding stations and may become daily visitors. Food preferences include millet, cracked corn, cracked wheat, suet, and bread crumbs.

The best-known of the crowned sparrows is the immaculate looking white-crowned sparrow, with its boldly marked head stripes and clear breast. Where the white-crowned nests along the Pacific Coast southward to southern California, there is a resident population which in fall and winter is augmented by other white-crowneds that have poured down from the north after the breeding season. It is no wonder that the white-crowned is one of the most common birds in winter at feeding stations in this region.

Along with the white-crowneds comes still another crowned sparrow. This is the very similar golden-crowned which nests as far north as Alaska and in winter keeps to the Far West. A golden crown patch bordered by black helps us discern this sparrow from the white-crowned. These two species will forage peacefully together at bird feeders where, if anything, the golden-crowned is the tamer of the two. A few do stray eastward and may be found almost anywhere in the western states in winter.

The white-throated sparrow is primarily a bird of the East, but has a breeding range that extends into the western provinces of Canada. It is regularly seen in winter in the Pacific states, southern Arizona, and New Mexico. Here it visits feeding stations along with its far western relatives. The usual sparrow foods suit these last three species. The white-crowned will sometimes respond to sliced apple and the golden-crowned has a taste for green matter as evidenced by its habit of eating the blossoms of some garden flowers.

Juncos

Juncos are plucky birds that often arrive with a snowfall, making them one of the first birds to announce the coming of winter. They cautiously approach our feeders, flitting their tails and showing their white outer tail feathers. Soon, however they will settle down to become regular patrons. Although "snow-bird" is an appropriate nickname for them, in the mountains they also come to feeders during the nesting season and look for tidbits at picnic areas and camping grounds.

Formerly the West could claim six junco species, all different enough in appearance to be given common and scientific names of their own. But the fact that interbreeding occurred among some of them suggested that they were not full species after all. Now only two species are recognized—the dark-eyed junco, found nearly everywhere in winter, and the yellow-eyed junco of southeastern Arizona and southwestern New Mexico. Slate-colored, Oregon, gray-headed, and white-winged juncos are now considered different forms of the dark-eyed junco.

But it takes years before old names are lost. This will be especially true of the Oregon junco, the common junco of the West which ranges far south and east of its breeding grounds in winter, when they are found through the Great Plains and some as far east as the Atlantic Coast. The Oregon junco is a striking bird with a jet black hood and breast that contrasts with white underparts, buffy or pink sides, and brown wings and back. It is the junco that is most familiar to bird feeders in the West, so it is perhaps too bad that it is now regarded only as a race of the widespread dark-eyed junco.

Not only do juncos eat the smaller seeds and grain in mixtures, but also sunflower seeds, suet, suet mixtures, bread, doughnuts, and food scraps of various kinds. Although they normally feed on the ground, they are able to learn how to balance themselves on perches of bird feeders to get at seed.

Blackbirds

The subfamily or group which includes the partly or wholly black birds also includes meadowlarks and orioles. The orioles have substantial amounts of yellow or orange in their plumages and have habits and behavior which differs from the other so-called blackbirds. Orioles favor habitats with scattered trees and often build their woven, pendant nests in the shade trees of towns and cities. Meadowlarks are open-country birds that rarely stray into built-up areas and seldom appear at bird feeders, except in bad weather. The blackbirds, grackles, and cowbirds, on the other hand, have discovered the best of both worlds. Although field foragers, they have also discovered that they can obtain a substantial share of their food within heavily populated districts. Foraging upon lawns, searching through trash, and in bad weather descending upon bird feeders in large numbers, the grackles, cowbirds, and Brewer's blackbirds find a good living.

The great-tailed grackle, well-established from Louisiana to California, is expanding its range northward into Utah and Colorado. The somewhat smaller common grackle is pushing its way westward from its range in the Great Plains. A waddling gait, glossy black plumage in the male, a long boat-shaped tail, and piercing yellow eyes tell us that we are looking at one of these invaders. They can be troublesome guests at bird feeders and are among the least popular of the blackbirds. As if aware of our low opinion of them, they tend to stay away except when snow cover or food shortage leave them with no other choice.

Not so different in appearance from the grackles is the smaller, more friendly Brewer's blackbird. Found everywhere in the West and in winter as far east as the southern Atlantic states, the Brewer's has established a special niche for itself in towns and cities. It patrols streets, sidewalks, parking lots, and drive-ins ever on the lookout for edible scraps discarded by humans. The rolls, bread, sandwiches, and popcorn it finds are better-liked, apparently, than most of the foods that are offered at feeding stations. Almost reluctantly they do come now and then to bird feeders to eat grain and tidbits of various kinds.

The cowbirds are represented by the bronzed cowbird of Texas and parts of the Southwest, and by the widely ranging brown-headed cowbird. Cowbirds are probably even less popular than the grackles. Because of their parasitic nest habits, cowbirds do not build their own nests. Instead, the female cowbird deposits her eggs in the nests of small songbirds—usually warblers or sparrows. The unwitting host parents raise the cowbird nestling as one of their own. The frequent result of this nest parasitism is that the true offspring of the host birds do not survive to fledge.

Like other blackbirds, cowbirds at times come to feeders in large numbers and take more than their share of the food. I discuss the problem of coping with cowbirds and grackles, as well as starlings and house sparrows in Chapter 13.

The red-winged blackbird is in a class by itself. Neither warmly welcomed nor, as a rule, disdained, the redwing is not overly troublesome at our feeders. Indeed, the male is often regarded as the first herald of spring. Arriving ahead of the females, males select perches and give vent to a cheerful sounding *konk-la-ree*. He is a handsome bird with his red or orange-red epaulets etched against an otherwise black plumage. Only when flocks of redwings arrive in fall or winter are feeders sometimes subject to overcrowding. Here they will eat a variety of seeds and other foods on the ground and or on platform feeders.

Red-winged blackbirds (male shown here) usually visit feeders in flocks.

Almost identical to the redwing is the uncommon tricolored blackbird, nesting in a few marshes in California and Oregon. Tricoloreds will sometimes come to feeders in coastal California.

Marshy wetlands in the West are the home of still another member of the blackbird family, the handsome yellow-headed blackbird, in which both the male and female sport a touch of yellow on their heads and breast. In the male, yellow covers the entire head and breast contrasting beautifully with the bird's mostly black plumage. Many of those who feed birds would like to see more of these stately-looking blackbirds. When flocks travel south in the fall, the birds usually disperse into grain fields and sometimes gather at corrals and stock pens in huge flocks to feed. As a rule, yellow-headeds visit feeders only in bad weather and seldom come in large numbers. But a yellow-headed that strays off course will sometimes settle for a yard that has bird feeders and may decide to spend the winter.

The blackbirds are content to eat less-expensive foods—cracked corn, wheat, oats, milo, other sorghums, rice, and bakery products. But if we let them, they will also make a dent in the sunflower supply, and suet and suet mixes. It helps to scatter cheaper foods on the ground and to keep more expensive ones in tubular hanging feeders since blackbirds will readily feed on the ground.

Grackles, redwings, and Brewer's blackbirds have a habit of taking food to the nearest water and wetting it before it is eaten. This seems to make the food easier to swallow or digest. The water treatment is usually reserved for drier foods like popcorn and bakery products, and the birdbath is commonly used for this purpose.

Orioles

No one has any hesitation about welcoming the orioles. Not only are they among the most colorful birds that visit feeders, but they have limited tastes and ordinarily do not come into competition with many of the other birds. Like hummingbirds and tanagers, they are with most of us only for the nesting season, and, for the most part, return to the tropics to spend the rest of the year. Three species occur widely in the West and three others are found only in border regions with Mexico. The best-known and most widespread of the orioles is the northern oriole. Like the dark-eyed junco, it has been combined or "lumped," in its case with one other, to make a single species. The strictly western Bullock's oriole was combined with the Baltimore oriole of the East to make the northern oriole. Many people in the West cling to the name Bullock's, and they soon may find that they were correct in doing so. The ornithologists who make the changes in nomenclature are reconsidering and may decide that the Bullock's and Baltimore are indeed separate species.

Of the three common orioles in the West, the Bullock's, to use the old name, ranges the farthest north and eats the greatest variety of foods. Ranging from southwestern Canada southward into Mexico, the Bullock's oriole is found nearly everywhere except at higher elevations. Besides insects and nectar from flowers, it accepts a wide variety of foods at bird feeders. Among those with special appeal are suet, suet mixes, softened raisins, grapes and grape jelly, grapefruit, orange, and watermelon. The Bullock's oriole also stays behind in winter more often than the others. In some areas it is not unusual to have a dozen coming to feeders at this time of the year. Summer can also be a busy time, when young accompanied by parents arrive to learn the technique of how to feed at hummingbird feeders or take full advantage of the other foods.

The hooded oriole, which breeds from northern California southward into Arizona, New Mexico, and southern Texas, is a brilliantly colored oriole—the male, like the Bullock's, is a contrasting black and orange-yellow. The breeding range of the hooded is closely tied to the presence of trees it favors for nesting purposes, primarily cottonwoods, eucalyptus, palms, and palmettos. The pendant nests of hooded orioles are often constructed entirely of fibers from palm leaves.

Like other orioles, the hooded visits the blossoms of flowers to obtain nectar. Instead of seeking nectar in the legitimate way by probing at the entrance to the flower, the hooded customarily punctures the base and therefore does not act as a pollinator. Agaves, aloes, and hibiscus are among the flowers that receive this treatment. Watermelon and sugar water are favorite foods in addition to those preferred by the Bullock's. The hooded can be expected in winter in very small numbers from southern California to southern Texas.

The Scott's oriole is the largest of the three common oriole species. It is a bird of the high desert and wooded canyons of the Southwest and ranges from southern California to western Texas. Wherever they are found, Scott's orioles are conspicuous, noisy birds whose melodious song rings out over the hot desert during the summer months. Yuccas and agaves are patronized for their nectar and sugar water feeders are highly favored. Fruits, including apricots, figs, peaches, and halved oranges, are well-received at bird feeders. A few Scott's orioles spend the winter in desert regions of southern California and in the more southern parts of Arizona and New Mexico.

Limited to southern Texas, but present there all year are the Altamira oriole and Audubon's oriole. The orchard oriole, primarily an eastern bird, is very common in summer in parts of western Texas and the Great Plains. And sugar water feeders in Arizona and California are occasionally visited by the streakbacked oriole, a rare stray from Mexico.

Finches

In contrast to species that have strong ties to the tropics, most of the finches have ranges that are dominantly northern and extend southward through the mountains. Many finches that nest farther south do not undertake long migrations to the tropics in the fall, traveling only as far as necessary to obtain food. Finches that nest at higher elevations make annual down-the-mountain (altitudinal) migrations to areas that offer better wintering conditions. These flights may be coupled with a limited movement southward. During some years the northern finches, as they are called, appear in greater numbers than usual and fan out into territory where they are rarely seen. These invasions are similar to those seen in the pinyon jay, Clark's nutcracker, varied thrush, and Bohemian waxwing. They appear to be triggered by poor food crops in the normal winter range. Population pressure resulting from a highly successful nesting season could also be a factor which forces finches to move.

When an invasion does occur, the finches inevitably come into contact with humans. Where food is offered, they throng to feeders so fearlessly that we worry about their safety. Because the northern finches have little experience with humans and our habitations, they appear to show complete confidence in us and seem unaware of the related dangers, such as from predation by cats. One observer, quoted in the Bent *Life Histories* series, tells how rosy finches fresh from the mountains greeted him when he appeared outside to refill the bird feeders; some of them perched upon his head and others walked over his shoes. Similar behavior is often displayed by the pine grosbeak, pine siskin, redpolls, and crossbills. With experience the birds learn of the dangers at our feeders and scatter when a cat or hawk approaches.

As far south as Arizona and New Mexico, the high mountains offer conditions similar to those that exist in Alaska and western Canada. The plant life and climate are much the same. (I discuss these habitat types or "life zones" in Chapter 7.) Among the northern finches that nest in the high mountains, even as far south as Arizona and New Mexico, are the pine grosbeak, rosy finch (New Mexico only), and evening grosbeak. The red crossbill, with one of the longest north-to-south ranges of any finch, nests from southwestern Alaska southward in the mountains all the way to Nicaragua.

When finches do visit feeding stations, they usually come in large numbers that can put a strain upon the larder. It is wise to have an extra supply of food on hand that will meet the needs of these seemingly famished diners when bad weather comes. The best food to offer is sunflower seeds. Black oil sunflower seed is nutritionally superior to striped sunflower, though both are readily consumed. There is more meat in proportion to shell in the black oil and the seeds are easier for the smaller-billed finches, such as the pine siskin, to open. The evening grosbeak is so partial to sunflower that it will rarely visit feeders for any other foods. For the smaller finches (siskins, goldfinches, redpolls, etc.), thistle seed (sometimes called "niger") is superior to anything we can offer. These tiny, oil-rich seeds are highly nutritious and will last much longer in the feeder than the much larger sunflower seeds because they are not consumed so easily. When thistle is offered in a special thistle feeder the finches can take only a small number of seeds at a time. This can mean a savings on the bird food bill, even though thistle seed is usually more expensive per pound than oil or striped sunflower.

Of the northern finches, none is more hardy in snow and frigid weather than the sparrow-sized rosy finch. Nesting from northern Alaska to above timberline in the southern Rockies, it is a bird that many people never see. But even these self-reliant birds are obliged to come down to the plains when conditions become too severe. Thousands may suddenly appear along roadsides and, rarely, in towns and cities. At such times they come to bird feeders in such numbers that other birds have difficulty eating. When the weather improves, the rosy finches usually leave.

Although the rosy finch is now regarded as a single species, there are five easily recognizable races—four of them once regarded as individual species. One of the most distinctive looking of the former species is the black rosy finch, entirely black except for a gray crown and prominent rose-pink in the wings. The rosy finch seen most commonly at bird feeders is the gray-crowned rosy finch, which is largely brown and with a gray crown and black forehead and rose-pink in the wings. At bird feeders the rosy finches respond well to smaller seeds, including canary seed, millet, and finely cracked corn. This food closely resembles the weed seeds they feed upon in the wild.

Largely indifferent to feeding station fare, the pine grosbeak stays in the mountains or the North as long as there is a good supply of seeds of mountain ash, pine, maple, and similar food plants. During invasion years these colorful grosbeaks travel southward into the northern Great Plains and farther only rarely. Following the example of other birds they sometimes visit

bird feeders and when they do, their favorite food by far is sunflower seed.

The purple finch is sometimes called a northern finch because it appears with the others during invasion years. However, this finch has a range that includes wide areas in Canada, a coastal belt stretching southward into California, and in the Cascades all the way to southern California. Winter invasions see it as far south as the Mexican border. The male is not truly purple, but raspberry red or wine-colored. At bird feeders, purple finches have a tendency to become highly belligerent among themselves. They seem to be cowed, however, when feeders are occupied by other finches, especially the house finch. Purple finches spend a long time shelling and eating sunflower seeds and, like other finches, they do their eating at the feeder. This is why so much congestion occurs when a flock of finches arrives. Purple finches are also fond of safflower, millet, and thistle seeds. They also sample suet and suet mixes.

The Cassin's finch breeds in the western mountains at higher elevations than the purple finch. Therefore it is less familiar at bird feeders except when it wanders to lower elevations after the breeding season. Like the purple finch, some travel as far as the Mexican border and beyond in winter. Close and careful study is necessary to separate the look-alike Cassin's, purple, and house finches from each other. Consult your field guide when in doubt. Cassin's finches have food preferences similar to the purple finch.

The house finch is often compared to the house sparrow because of its ability to live close to humans and to occupy many of the same niches. If either of these two birds is winning the

battle for the same foods and nesting sites, it is the house finch.
Within recent years the house finch, a species native to much of
the West, has experienced a phenomenal range expansion and
the end is not yet in sight. A small introduced population in the
New York City region began to increase and move into adjoining
states during the 1950s and 1960s. Presently the descendants are
breeding throughout much of the East and have already crossed
the Mississippi, so eastern and western populations may soon
meet. In the West, house finches are found nearly everywhere
except at very high elevations. Since 1930, they have colonized
eastward into Texas and northward from California into Oregon, Washington, and British Columbia. These finches were first
observed in Vancouver, British Columbia in 1935.

This population explosion has come at the expense of the
house sparrow at a time when this overbearing bird was already
decreasing in numbers—drastically so in the East. This is evident
at bird feeders and in farmyards where the trend is ever more
house finches and fewer house sparrows. This is good news for
those who prefer a more colorful bird with a pleasing song. At
the same time, there is some concern that the house finch may
have some of the faults of the house sparrow. It does tend to
monopolize bird feeders. Other small finches, especially goldfinches and purple finches, go elsewhere when they find that the
competition is too severe.

One of the reasons for the house finch's success is its nearly
omnivorous diet. To the chagrin of fruit growers, house finches
have a habit of nibbling at ripe fruits, spoiling more than they
eat. Among the fruits that are attacked are peaches, plums, apricots, figs, loquats, and grapes. However, a large share of their
diet consists of weed seeds, including those of wild mustard and
dandelion. Nearly every food offered at bird feeders appeals to
these undiscriminating eaters. Watermelon, cantaloupe, sunflower (especially hulled sunflower seeds), and thistle seed are
at the top of the list. Other foods include millet, rape, canary
seed, suet, doughnuts, raisins, pomegranate, apples, and dates.
Along with hummingbirds and orioles, house finches are among
the most eager visitors to sugar water feeders.

A redeeming trait for those who find house finches troublesome is that they are seldom steady visitors to bird feeders since
natural foods, on the whole, take precedence over those at feeders. One of the times when house finches are most numerous at
feeders is when parents bring their young during the nesting
season. After young are on their own, there is a dispersal which

may see some of the birds moving to new territory. However, the house finches we see in the West are basically non-migratory and will be present in varying numbers throughout the year.

With their crossed mandibles—for which they are named—crossbills are highly specialized birds that rarely feed upon anything other than the seeds of cone-bearing plants. They use their bills expertly to extract the seeds of conifers, spruces, and other trees. The red crossbill will leave the mountains and northern woods during times of poor seed crops, appearing as far south as the border regions with Mexico.

The white-winged crossbill participates in the same movements but does not travel as far to the south. Sunflower is about the only food that attracts either of the crossbills to a feeder. Once onto sunflower seed at bird feeders, crossbills become persistent guests and exhibit the extraordinary tameness seen in other northern birds that have had few contacts with humans.

Among the northern finches, only the redpolls nest as far north and are as well adapted to the cold of northern winters as the rosy finches. Redpolls are small birds, only five to five-and-a-half inches in length. There is nothing in their appearance to suggest that they are so rugged. The redpolls have red caps (or "polls"), black chins, streaked grayish bodies, and tinges of pink in their plumages. Hoary and common redpolls, both of which nest in the arctic regions of Alaska and Canada, look almost exactly alike, the hoary having a slightly paler coloration. The hoary is the less common of the two species and does not travel as far south during invasion years. The common redpoll may appear as far south as Oregon, northern Utah, Colorado, and Nebraska. Keeping to the open country and traveling in large flocks, the redpolls search for weed seeds. Flocks will visit bird feeders as fearlessly as do the other northern finches. Foods that are preferred include sunflower, suet, millet, canary seed, flax seed, and bread.

While similar to the redpolls in habits and behavior, the pine siskin differs from its far-northern cousins by nesting as far south as the mountains of western Texas, New Mexico, and Arizona. Nomadic wanderers, like so many of the other finches, they search for food at lower elevations after the nesting season. They move from one source to another, seldom being held in one place even by inexhaustible supplies at bird feeders.

In the wild the siskins feed upon seeds of conifers, alders, and birches, as well as a variety of weed seeds. At bird feeders they are feisty birds picking quarrels and sometimes snatching food from the very beaks of larger birds. The siskins refuse to tolerate the presence of house sparrows at the same feeders. Giving way to the siskin's sharp bills and ferocious attacks, the sparrows leave and seldom come back as long as siskins are in the area.

Pine siskins also act as gleaners at bird feeders, searching through tidbits left behind by other birds. At the same time, they feed eagerly upon thistle seeds, black oil sunflower (which they can usually open), suet, suet mixes, millet, nut meats, and rolled oats. Despite their feeder etiquette, they are often favorites with those who feed birds.

Although 'northern' is a far less appropriate word to use in referring to the goldfinches, these birds have much the same habits as redpolls and siskins and are equally popular at bird feeders. Seed eaters, specializing in seeds of garden plants and weeds, the goldfinches throng to places where there is a good source of food.

The wide-ranging American goldfinch, which nests across northern North America is attracted to ripe seeds of both wild and cultivated sunflowers, wild thistles, bachelor's button, coreopsis, dandelion, marigold, zinnia, sweet rocket, rosemary, scarlet sage, cosmos, chicory, and hollyhock. So dependent is the American goldfinch upon ample supplies of food of this kind, especially the wild thistle, that it waits until the height of the harvest in late summer before nesting. If favorite foods are available at bird feeders, full advantage is taken of them regardless of the season. There have been occasions when I had no goldfinches at all at my feeders but I soon had flocks of American goldfinches coming, after hanging a thistle feeder full of seeds. Sunflower seeds, as well as suet, suet mixes, canary seeds, millet, and nut meats are popular at feeders.

The lesser goldfinch is not nearly so responsive. On the whole, this western goldfinch is much more southern in distribution, found in two forms from southwestern Washington to central Texas. A black-backed form ranges all the way into northern South America, while green-backed birds are predominant in the western United States. The dietary habits of the lesser goldfinch are much the same as those of the American, but somehow the birds do not take to our feeders as readily. Water, more than food, brings them to the yard.

Even less expected at our feeders is the Lawrence's goldfinch, which comes close to being an exclusively California species. This least brightly colored of the goldfinches is also found in southern parts of Arizona and New Mexico in some winters. It would be a triumph to attract even one of these shy birds to a bird feeder, but few people have succeeded.

Like other seed eaters, the goldfinches are obliged to supplement their diet with ample amounts of water. That is why they are so often seen drinking at puddles and birdbaths. Having had a drink, they almost invariably go on to indulge in a round of bathing.

Compared to the smaller finches, the evening grosbeak has a comparatively huge, conical bill, ideally suited for crushing and removing hard outer shells or husks. Even the hard pits of cherries are crushed between the mandibles and the kernels extracted. When eating sunflower seeds at bird feeders, evening grosbeaks are capable of shelling and eating as many as 100 seeds in as little as five minutes. It is no wonder that the supply quickly vanishes when a whole flock is feeding. In the wild the grosbeaks feast upon samaras of maples and other trees with winged seed cases, also some fruits, and even seeds as small as those of the apple.

There is little conflict between the grosbeak's diet and that of smaller finches. The latter use their bills to gather the seeds of weeds, garden plants, and wild plants, such as alder and birch. Only when it comes to sunflower is there likely to be any conflict. Evening grosbeaks accept little else at bird feeders but sunflower, and many times refuse these seeds in favor of wild ones.

In summer, both in the western mountains and more northern parts of its breeding range, evening grosbeaks sometimes appear at feeders along with newly fledged young. Sunflower continues to be the favored food, although millet, sorghum, and safflower may also be taken. Both in summer and winter, evening grosbeaks and other finches seem to have a craving for something that is missing from their dominantly vegetarian diets. A supply of grit and certain minerals which act as aids to digestion seems to be the answer. This is why these birds are often seen getting salty earth at roadsides and around salt blocks for cattle. They will also consume small amounts of sand, pieces of charcoal or even dry earth. Placing a small container of very small, dry pebbles or sand may help to attract these seed eaters to your feeding station.

Water is equally important. An ice-free birdbath is one of the best provisions we can make for evening grosbeaks and other finches in winter. ☐

Feeder Birds

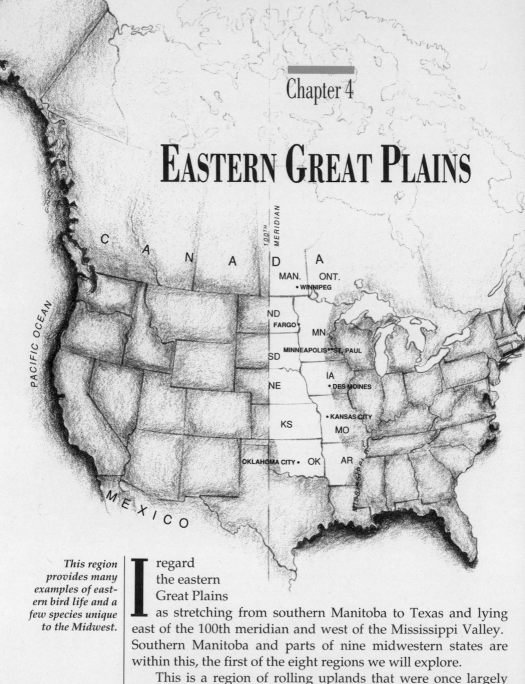

Chapter 4

EASTERN GREAT PLAINS

This region provides many examples of eastern bird life and a few species unique to the Midwest.

I regard the eastern Great Plains as stretching from southern Manitoba to Texas and lying east of the 100th meridian and west of the Mississippi Valley. Southern Manitoba and parts of nine midwestern states are within this, the first of the eight regions we will explore.

This is a region of rolling uplands that were once largely open prairie but that over the years have been greatly altered by human beings. Towns and cities have sprung up, trees have been planted, highways and rail lines built, and much of the land converted to agriculture and grazing.

To some the West evokes the Hollywood images of cattle

ranches and cowboys. To the bird watcher, the West means magpies, yellow-headed blackbirds, and roadrunners. But how far west do we have to look before the bird life, together with the scenery, begins to take on a distinctly western flavor?

According to Roger Tory Peterson, in his *Field Guide to the Birds East of the Rockies*, the 100th meridian forms a rough dividing line between eastern and western avifauna. A north-to-south line, the meridian bisects parts of the states of North and South Dakota, Nebraska, Kansas, Oklahoma, and Texas. Peterson does not mean to suggest that western birds suddenly appear and that eastern species disappear from the landscape west of the meridian. Only slowly, almost imperceptibly does the landscape and bird life change across the Great Plains. About all that one can say about the 100th meridian is that a few more western birds make an appearance as the landscape becomes more open and towns and cities are ever farther apart.

*Harris' sparrow
at a winter feeder.*

A corridor lying half way across the continent, the eastern Great Plains is really a mixture of East and West. Although the avifauna is predominantly eastern, there are enough western birds to make this a meeting place. This is where the closely related black-headed and rose-breasted grosbeaks meet and sometimes interbreed. Here, too, eastern and western meadowlark ranges meet. These two birds look almost exactly alike and can be safely distinguished only by their very different songs. Before Bullock's and Baltimore orioles (now the northern oriole) were lumped into a single species, the ranges of the two meet on the Great Plains. The same is true of yellow-shafted and red-shafted flickers (now lumped to form the northern flicker).

In winter, the eastern Great Plains shares the Harris' sparrow with neighboring parts of the Midwest. This distinctive sparrow, which nests in the Far North, has a very definite mid-continent wintering range which is only about 100 miles wide and 300 miles long. Another middle American species, the dickcissel, nests in the eastern Great Plains but travels far to the south in winter. A few always stay behind and disperse widely in several directions.

Add a few typically western birds, like the scissor-tailed flycatcher and western kingbird that breed, and the greater roadrunner, a year-round resident, and it becomes clear that the eastern Great Plains is a mixture of East and West.

A few birds widely regarded as western have ranges that extend well into the East. The western meadowlark, for example, nests sparingly as far east as the eastern Great Lakes region and the Brewer's blackbird breeds as far east as Michigan and southern Ontario. More common in the West than the East, Bewick's wren has a breeding range that extends as far east as the western edge of the Appalachian Mountains.

Birds to expect at feeders in the eastern Great Plains region vary somewhat from north to south. In more northern portions the winter will almost certainly see evening grosbeaks, common redpolls, and possibly pine grosbeaks at feeders. In more southern portions these northern birds will rarely appear—their place taken by species such as the red-bellied woodpecker, mockingbird, and cardinal.

Eastern Oklahoma

A winter bird feeder survey by the Nongame Program of the Oklahoma Department of Wildlife Conservation provides a good picture of birds to expect in the southern portion during January. Reports from 2,211 respondents who tallied the birds at their feeders for two consecutive days in January, 1988, showed the American goldfinch to be the most common feeder visitor, followed in descending order by the dark-eyed junco, cardinal, starling, red-winged blackbird, blue jay, Carolina chickadee, Harris' sparrow, tufted titmouse, and house sparrow. A total of 45 species were recorded altogether and of these only three—western meadowlark, Brewer's blackbird, and Harris' sparrow—could be said to have predominantly western ranges.

According to the survey, most bird feeding was conducted in urban areas. Yards were generally larger than three-fourths of an acre and well-planted with trees and shrubs. This survey also seemed to indicate that the presence of natural food did not deter birds from visiting feeders.

Where feeding is conducted all year and sugar water is offered in summer, we once again find that eastern species predominate. Luann Waters, who lives south of Oklahoma City, attracts three species not recorded in the January survey: ruby-throated hummingbird and northern oriole in summer, and northern bobwhite at almost any season. Her feeders are visited by 21 species, including such expected ones as mourning dove, blue jay, purple finch, pine siskin, and American goldfinch.

John Skeen, who feeds birds in a suburb of Oklahoma City, can claim the same birds that come to Ms. Waters's feeders as well as 13 others. Less common visitors to his feeders include the brown creeper, rusty blackbird, and house finch. The latter is still uncommon in eastern Oklahoma. But as this prolific finch presses westward from the Mississippi Valley and eastward from the Great Plains, the region will soon experience the same kind of house finch population boom that has taken place elsewhere.

Luann Waters and John Skeen, experienced bird feeders who are both employed by the Oklahoma Department of Wildlife Conservation, offer birds sunflower, millet, cracked corn, suet and suet mixtures. In summer fruit and sugar water are provided. According to the survey, these foods, along with thistle seed, are the most commonly offered by those who feed birds in Oklahoma.

The importance of water was also emphasized by the winter bird survey, which found that *the most active feeders were those closest to a source of water*.

The North-Central States and Manitoba

A comparison of winter bird feeder surveys conducted in Oklahoma, Kansas, and Iowa shows that all three states record large numbers of American goldfinches, dark-eyed juncos, northern cardinals, chickadees, tufted titmice, and blue jays. One difference is that the Carolina chickadee found in Oklahoma is replaced by the black-capped chickadee in Kansas and Iowa. Woodpeckers, including downy, red-headed, red-bellied, and the northern flicker, are more common in Kansas and Iowa and northward. The Harris' sparrow, the eighth most common bird at Oklahoma feeders, drops to 12th place in Kansas and 19th place in Iowa.

In terms of birds sometimes regarded as a nuisance at feeders, the house sparrow is the most common feeder patron in Kansas, third most common one in Iowa, and the tenth most

This busy yard attracts cardinals, chickadees, tufted titmice, and other birds of the eastern Great Plains.

common in Oklahoma. The European starling is common at feeders in Oklahoma and Kansas, but less so in Iowa. The common grackle is just below the house sparrow in attendance at Oklahoma feeders, but absent in Kansas, and all but absent in Iowa. Two others, the red-winged blackbird and brown-headed cowbird, are common at feeders in Oklahoma but nearly absent in Kansas and Iowa.

In these surveys there are a few examples of northern species which visit feeders during the winter months. Pine siskins are common visitors to feeders in Kansas and Iowa and much less common in Oklahoma. Iowa has a monopoly on ring-necked pheasants and common redpolls, and also has the majority of purple finches which visited feeders.

North of the border, in Manitoba, much more striking seasonal differences are seen at feeding stations. Instead of being a winter resident, the Harris' sparrow, en route between its far northern breeding grounds, is only a spring and fall transient in southern Manitoba. Here there are fewer species and fewer birds in winter. By late fall most of the American goldfinches, pine siskins, and dark-eyed juncos have traveled south for the winter. Most members of the blackbird family have departed and the starling ranks have become depleted. But the house sparrow, a permanent resident, stays on to brave the snow and cold of winter. Many do not survive if the weather is overly harsh. The northern cardinal, present in small numbers in southern Manitoba, also remains behind in winter. The few that are present may become highly dependent upon food at feeding stations in severe weather. Much the same is true of the mourning doves that stay behind. But hardy species like the hairy and downy woodpecker, blue jay, black-capped chickadee, white-breasted nuthatch, Bohemian waxwing, evening grosbeak, pine grosbeak, common and hoary redpoll, purple finch, and snow bunting are undaunted by the cold. It would have to be a harsh winter indeed to force many of these birds to go south. Lack of food rather than cold can result in a mass exodus during some years. When this occurs, it is called an "invasion" by those who see the birds farther south and in greater numbers than usual.

The game bird seen most commonly near feeders and in farmland in southern Manitoba is the gray partridge, an introduced species that is more hardy than the ring-necked pheasant. Along with native sharp-tailed, spruce, and ruffed grouse, it is a bird to look for in some northern states and southern provinces of Canada, since any one of these game birds may appear around farmsteads looking for food if hard-pressed in winter.

The blue jay is the most common feeder bird in and around the capital city of Winnipeg, Manitoba, according to Mrs. Jean Bancroft, who has been feeding birds for more than 30 years. Besides the blue jay, her most dependable guests include the mourning dove, downy and hairy woodpeckers, black-capped chickadee, white-breasted nuthatch, house sparrow, starling, common grackle, purple finch, and evening grosbeak, and in summer, northern oriole and rose-breasted grosbeak. She uses a birdseed mixture containing sunflower, milo, wheat, millet, rape, and canary seed. She also provides halved orange for fruit eaters.

Mrs. E. R. Taylor, a friend of Mrs. Bancroft who feeds birds at Grand Marais on Lake Winnipeg, has many of the same birds at her feeders. Like Mrs. Bancroft she plays host to hairy and downy woodpeckers, evening grosbeaks, American goldfinches, and white-breasted nuthatches. Less regular visitors include Harris' sparrows during migration and a yellow warbler that hovers before her sugar water in much the same way as a hummingbird.

The one hummingbird that commonly visits feeders in Manitoba is the ruby-throated, which arrives from the tropics in the middle of May. Both Mrs. Bancroft and Mrs. Taylor recommend columbine, nasturtium, salvia, gladiolus, delphinium, and petunia as plants which will provide natural sources of nectar for the rubythroats.

For fruit and berry eaters, including the American robin and cedar and Bohemian waxwings, they recommend mountain ash, cotoneaster, wild cherry, Virginia creeper, crabapple, and serviceberry or saskatoon (*Amelanchier*), as it is commonly called in Canada.

Hummingbirds

Although hummingbirds from the West do reach the region, the single species that breeds and stays through the summer is the ruby-throated. Among the flowers that do well in the region and are especially inviting to the ruby-throated are those of the buckeye (*Aesculus glabra*), glossy abelia, mimosa (*Albizzia julibrissin*), penstemon, bee balm, cardinal flower, columbine, Indian paintbrush (*Castilleja coccinea*), prickly pear (*Opuntia*), and salvia, among many others. The ruby-throated, like other hummingbirds, shows a preference for red or brightly colored flowers, especially those that are tubular in shape, and which, of course, produce nectar.

In southern portions of the plains, hot, dry summers, below

freezing temperatures in winter, and alkaline soil limit the number of plants that do well. The best advice I can offer on bird food plants, as well as birdhouses, is to send for a free copy of *Attracting Birds*, published by the Oklahoma Department of Wildlife Conservation (1801 N. Lincoln Blvd., Oklahoma City, OK 73105). The information contained in this brochure will be useful wherever one attracts birds in the eastern Great Plains region.

To mention a few of the plants that the ODWC recommends, one can't go wrong with box elder, hackberry, mulberry, the hawthorns, deciduous holly (*Ilex decidua*), elderberry, multiflora rose, and the dogwoods. Although some of these plants are not ideal from an ornamental standpoint, they are good suppliers of food for birds.

Birdhouses

The agricultural and rural regions of the eastern Great Plains are home to one of our best-loved birds, the eastern bluebird. Bluebirds are not only beautiful in plumage and song, they are beneficial to us because of the many insects they consume. Eastern bluebirds, which nest throughout the eastern Great Plains are fairly easy to attract to birdhouses if we offer the right type of house in the right habitat.

Among the best places to put up houses for bluebirds are roadsides in open country, field edges, and near clearings. In open country the birds are freer of competition from house sparrows and starlings and are better able to find the insects and berries upon which they live. Bluebird houses should be placed on fence posts or other structures at a height of only three or four feet from the ground. Bluebird trails with many hundreds of houses have been established within the range of the eastern bluebird and farther west where they are used by western and mountain bluebirds. Persons establishing bluebird trails along roads adjoining private lands should always obtain permission from landowners before placing houses.

During the nesting season many species other than bluebirds may use the nestboxes, such as tree swallows, chickadees, tufted titmice, white-breasted nuthatches, and Bewick's wrens. Some bluebird trail operators prefer to remove these other species before they nest to give the bluebirds a better chance at nesting success. Most people, however welcome these small birds if they build in the houses, since they too need places to nest. Larger houses can also be provided for birds such as woodpeckers, owls, and wood ducks.

The eastern Great Plains is also purple martin country. In contrast to the bluebird, the purple martin prefers to nest near human habitations. So long as a yard is reasonably open, there is a good chance of attracting martins with apartment-type houses or hollowed-out gourds with entrance holes. Attracting birds to houses is easy if directions for placement and maintenance are carefully followed. Consult one of the many birdhouse books available commercially for detailed instructions on house construction, placement, and maintenance. You'll find this is an enjoyable extension of your feeding activities.

Special Problems

Both in Manitoba and in the plains states to the south, many feeding stations are plagued by the so-called "nuisance" species: the house sparrow, starling, cowbird, grackle, and red-winged blackbird. These species, when they descend upon our feeders in large flocks, often limit easy access by other feeder birds. This is a problem nearly everywhere that birds are fed, but in the grain-growing belt of the Midwest it is somewhat more acute. Plentiful food supplies, both natural and agricultural, allow these species to increase in numbers to the point where they are a nuisance in towns and cities, and any place where bird feeding is conducted. While the house sparrow is a resident near human habitation, the others do most of their feeding in grain fields. But when snow covers the source of supply or bitter cold sets in, the field foragers know where to go to find food: our feeding stations. As a rule, their visits to bird feeders last only as long as the weather remains unsuitable for normal feeding. When the emergency is over they return to the fields again.

Bluebird houses should be mounted four feet off the ground, with predator guards in place.

Using lethal methods to solve these problems is not necessary, can be dangerous for us and for other species, and doesn't work effectively anyway. A happy compromise can be reached by using different, less expensive foods to meet the needs of field foragers. Scattering this cheaper seed on the ground while offering the usual foods in hanging feeders for the other birds we are able to feed all species easily. See Chapter 13, "Questions People Ask," for suggestions on how to adapt your feeding station to meet the needs of all birds.

Those who take up bird feeding should pursue their hobby with the intention of helping all hungry animals, not just those we decide that we like the most. At the same time, it is only fair to the smaller birds, and to native species, that they receive their proper share of the bounty at our feeders and in our yards. □

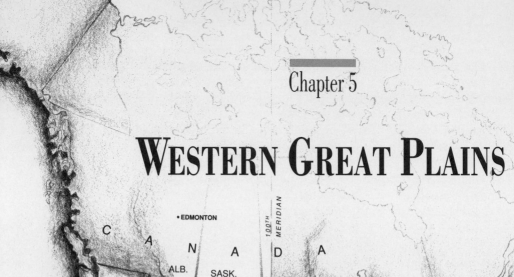

Chapter 5

WESTERN GREAT PLAINS

EDMONTON

100TH MERIDIAN

C A N A D A

ALB.   SASK.

MT
HELENA

ND

SD
RAPID CITY

WY   CASPER

NE

CHEYENNE

DENVER

CO   KS

PACIFIC OCEAN

ROCKY MOUNTAINS

M E X I C O

This region includes the lands west of the 100th meridian to the foothills of the Rockies.

Looking across the Great Plains, with its limitless horizons, it is easy to picture the way the land looked before the coming of the European explorers and settlers. The flat-topped mesas and sagebrush-covered hillsides are the same, as are the cottonwoods along the streams. But where vast herds of bison, or buffalo, once roamed, there are now endless wheat fields and ranchlands. The brown-headed cowbird follows the cattle as it once did the bison. Scissor-tailed flycatchers and western kingbirds perch on utility wires and ravens build their nests in steel towers that support high voltage lines. Although humans have left their mark, the bird life is still much the same.

The Black Hills

Driving westward one year in mid-November, toward Rapid City in the Black Hills of southwestern South Dakota, I began seeing western birds about halfway across the state. There was no question about the black-billed magpies and western meadowlarks along the roadsides, but a combination of rain and snow made it difficult for me to identify smaller birds I spotted some distance from the road. I decided that the flocks I was seeing were probably made up of horned larks, Lapland longspurs, and perhaps other longspur species as well.

Rapid City, South Dakota, at an elevation of over 3,000 feet, is well west of the 100th meridian. If you were to travel from east to west across the meridian, upon reaching Rapid City, you would note that the bird life now comprises predominately western species. In this regard, this is a transition area, much like the Edwards Plateau in south-central Texas.

Horned larks are year-round residents of the Great Plains.

The Black Hills, with peaks rising to over 6,000 feet, can be regarded as an eastern outpost of the Rocky Mountains, since many of the plants and birds are the same in the two regions. The Black Hills are also the main stronghold of the "white-winged" race of the dark-eyed junco, a pale gray bird with white wingbars, formerly considered a full species.

The Townsend's solitaires that occasionally appear at bird feeders in Rapid City are essentially wilderness birds. As their name suggests, they avoid close company—a single bird perched at the tip-top of a spruce or pine tree is a much more common sight than two or three together. Much more gregarious are the red-headed woodpeckers that frequent oak trees of the lower mountain slopes. They spend much of their time gathering and storing acorns and only rarely appear at feeders.

The summer months in this region offer such true western species as the mountain bluebird, western tanager, black-headed grosbeak, and lazuli bunting. Still, bird feeders in the western Great Plains at any time of year will likely be visited by greater numbers of species from the East than from the West.

Where the Rockies Begin

At the eastern edge of the Great Plains there is no visible topographical feature announcing a change in biotic provinces. But at the western edge, there is an abrupt change in elevation from near mile-high plains to foothills and, behind them, mountain peaks that rise to 13,000 feet and more. Early settlers favored the plains over the mountains as a place to build, as is evident in the presence of such cities as Denver, Colorado, Cheyenne, Wyoming, and Helena, Montana, at the eastern edge of the Rockies. The cities have the advantages of flat terrain, plentiful water, and an invigorating climate. For those who feed birds, they offer a mixture of plains and mountain species.

Denver

Denver, at an altitude of one mile above sea level, is within the Upper Sonoran Life Zone and therefore has a breeding bird population that differs considerably from that of the higher elevation Transition Zone immediately to the west. (See Chapter 7 for a discussion of the life zone concept.) But in fall and winter, when mountain birds descend to the plains, the tempo at feeding stations increases. And, if it is one of the years when "invaders" from the north or mountains appear in large numbers, Denverites can be hard-pressed to supply enough food to satisfy the hungry birds.

One of these winter visitors, the horned lark, is more of a plains than a mountain species. Arthur C. Bent, in his *Life Histories of North American Birds*, writes of horned larks in Colorado when snow covered their food supplies: "They congregate about the ranches and farmyards to feed on waste grain or come into the towns and cities to be fed by the residents. . . thousands of the birds come into the towns; there people feed them regularly on millet and other seeds, scattered on bare spaces. The birds often gather so thickly as to almost cover the ground."

Arriving from the north in huge numbers some years, Bohemian waxwings strip the fruit from ornamental trees and shrubs, and, if offered suitable fare, turn to handouts from residents. In Chapter 3, I described a record invasion during the winter of 1916-17 when thousands of the waxwings appeared in Denver and other cities and were fed raisins and canned peas. In Denver, the evening grosbeak, which is regarded as an invasion species in the Southwest, is both a resident and a winter visitor. But it appears in some winters in much greater numbers than in others. This is also true of the American goldfinch and pine siskin, both breeding birds, which appear in greater numbers in fall and winter. The Cassin's finch, which nests at higher altitudes, is a fall and winter visitor. On the other hand, its close relative, the house finch, is a year around resident, and, like the house sparrow, can be too numerous for the comfort of some of those who feed birds. But most complaints are reserved for dark-plumaged birds, like crows, magpies, starlings, blackbirds, and grackles.

Among the dependable guests that everyone likes at Denver feeders are downy and hairy woodpeckers, black-capped and mountain chickadees, white-breasted nuthatches, dark-eyed juncos, and white-crowned and song sparrows. The mountain chickadee and several races of juncos are present only in winter at this lower elevation.

To the northwest in nearby Boulder, at an altitude of 5,500 feet, Stephen Frye runs the Wild Bird Center and has informed me about the birds that come to several area feeding stations. Boulder has all the birds that visit feeders in Denver, and since it lies at the edge of the foothills, has greater prospects of receiving mountain birds like the scrub jay, Steller's jay, Clark's nutcracker, and pine grosbeak. As an example of how significant life zones can be in this part of the West, Mr. Frye tells me that the broad-tailed hummingbird is a common summer resident in the foothills and mountains west of Boulder. People who feed hummingbirds at these locations west of the Great Plains may have as many as 40 broad-taileds at their feeders at a time, consuming as much as a quart of sugar water a day. Yet in the lowlands east of Boulder, the broad-tailed is all but unknown.

As Mr. Frye has explained, with the planting of trees and green lawns, and with irrigation, towns and cities within the western Great Plains offer habitat conditions similar to those found in the Midwest. As a consequence, species once regarded

The broad-tailed hummingbird is common in the eastern foothills of the Rocky Mountains.

as eastern, have crossed the plains and reached the Rockies and beyond. This means that in addition to birds regarded as western, feeding stations are likely to be patronized by pioneer species such as the red-headed woodpecker, blue jay, rose-breasted grosbeak, and northern cardinal.

Wyoming and Montana

Northward from Denver, the Rockies bend westward, thereby making room for the Great Plains to extend farther to the west. In Wyoming, Casper and Sheridan are west of Denver but still well within the Great Plains. The same is true of Helena and Great Falls in Montana, which are roughly 700 miles northwest of Denver and are at elevations of 4,000 and 3,300 feet respectively.

Differences in birdlife are apparent, represented by the more northerly latitude and somewhat lower elevation. The variety of hummingbirds, especially during migration, is greater. Feeders in these regions may be visited by the Calliope and rufous hummers. The house finch is largely absent and is replaced by purple and Cassin's finches. Chances of having the western tanager and lazuli bunting at the bird feeder are greater. In winter, rosy finches are more common far out on the plains and sometimes appear in such numbers at bird feeders that they remind one of the pigeons in city parks that flock around anyone who is offering food.

Esther McWilliams in Sheridan tells how a few years ago she had only a few of these finches at her feeders. Now so many arrive in winter that she can hardly supply enough food to meet their needs. It takes several hundred pounds of sunflower, millet, and chick feed to see them through the winter. Along with magpies, which quickly consume the suet, the numbers coming to her feeders are "too much of a good thing," as she calls it.

At his farm near Gillette in northeastern Wyoming, Andy D. Jensen not only feeds hundreds of rosy finches in winter but also horned larks and wild turkeys. The last two forage for food in the barnyard and also visit the yard to pick up food below the bird feeders. Mr. Jensen has no objection to the not-so-wild turkeys outside his windows, but he wishes they would stick to whole corn and wheat instead of the more expensive sunflower. During the spring flocks of lark buntings appear in the barnyard and feed upon the undigested grain they find in horse manure. He supplements this diet with whole corn and red winter wheat.

The rosy finches—gray-crowned race—are the prime attraction at Mr. Jensen's feeders. Photos that accompanied Mr.

Jensen's correspondence show his grandson seated amid a flock of the birds. One of the finches is perched upon the boy's cap, and another is feeding on sunflower seeds at a plate he is holding. The ground nearby is so covered with feeding rosy finches that it is easy to see why these sparrow-sized birds have a reputation for over-running bird feeders. Mr. Jensen says he can't over-emphasize the importance of keeping cats under control where birds are as tame as the rosy finches at his feeders.

Mrs. Wayne Eveland in Helena makes sure that she does not miss any of the expected birds in her part of Montana. She offers a wide variety of foods at a number of feeders, and birdbaths, including a rock waterfall and a small pond. Every bird, no matter the species, that comes her way receives a warm welcome. After looking at her list of feeder birds, I wrote asking her if she did not have serious problems of competition between large birds and small ones or between closely related species. She admitted that smaller birds leave when magpies, Clark's nutcrackers, or jays arrive, but that the larger birds are not aggressive and the smaller ones quickly reappear when they leave. The Steller's jay is the common feeder species, whereas the gray jay is an infrequent visitor, as are flocks of pinyon jays. As for three species of nuthatches and two species of chickadees, they seem to time their visits well so that there is little conflict. Pygmy nuthatches arrive in small flocks at different times than the less sociable white-breasted and red-breasted nuthatches. Mountain and black-capped chickadees get along well together and come "in a constant flow" when she calls them. They love waffles, she states, and will eat pieces from her hand.

A mystery she never solved was why an American dipper from a nearby lake used to bob up and down on her deck railing just outside whatever room she was in. It did this for several months, though she never saw it eat anything at her feeders. My guess is that something on her varied menu appealed to the dipper and that its strange behavior was perhaps a way of asking for more.

Others who feed birds in Helena have much the same birds as Mrs. Eveland. Mrs. Charlotte McKibben has so many birds coming for food that she maintains seven feeders on her deck and one on a tree through the summer and adds three more in winter. In order to keep the birds well supplied with water, she has three birdbaths in summer and two heated ones in winter. She welcomes all the birds that come to her yard, even, begrudgingly, the pygmy-owls and goshawks that prey on her feeder birds.

Saskatchewan and Alberta

As far north as Edmonton in Alberta and Saskatoon in Saskatchewan, where several of our correspondents live, there are so few birds in winter that all are welcomed. Ernie Kuyt writes, "We have so few species in Edmonton that we do not mind the house sparrows. Some days that's all we see!" That house sparrows survive where it is too difficult for even juncos to spend the winter is a tribute to this hardy little bird's endurance. But there are occasions when the house sparrows succumb to the cold.

For those who think they know exactly how many birds of any species come to their feeders, Robert Carroll of Fort Saskatchewan, near Edmonton, has a word of caution. He writes, "On the past four Christmas Bird Counts, I've put down between 10 and 12 black-capped chickadees—the number I thought were visiting our feeders. Last week a local bird bander set up his nets at our feeders and banded 39 chickadees and that wasn't all of them. And I thought I knew exactly how many there were!" It is safe to say that many people underestimate the number of birds coming to their feeders. Birds have evolved to become highly mobile in their feeding practices. It is not general knowledge that after a busy session of feeding most birds leave and in time other birds arrive to take their place.

As far west as Saskatchewan and Alberta, one would expect the bird life to be distinctly western. Yet, except for black-billed magpies, the winter feeder birds in Edmonton and Saskatoon could have been copied from a list compiled in New York State or New England. Aside from the house sparrow, the two most expected species are the black-capped chickadee and blue jay. A little less common are downy and hairy woodpeckers, white and red-breasted nuthatches, and irruptive birds like evening and pine grosbeaks, crossbills, and pine siskins, which may be present in numbers some winters and absent in others.

This invasion by eastern species into Saskatchewan, Alberta, and even Alaska and British Columbia is the result of events which took place after the glaciers receded. With the warming of the climate, trees began growing in the once-icy north, but to the south, in the Great Plains, it was too dry for forests. Therefore, tree-loving birds, like woodpeckers, titmice, nuthatches, and the brown creeper were able to expand their ranges westward only via a northern route. This they did, and many moved

as far west as the Pacific Coast, among them, downy and hairy woodpeckers, and black-capped chickadees. With settlement and the planting of trees, the Great Plains area has now become a route for westward range expansion by eastern species.

Food

Sunflower seeds are the most popular food by far among those surveyed in the western Great Plains. Black oil sunflower seed was the variety that everyone used and preferred. Second in terms of popularity was white proso millet, and not far behind, white-striped sunflower, other millets, mixed birdseeds, suet, and niger. These findings were closely similar to those obtained by FeederWatch (an annual bird feeding survey conducted by the Cornell Laboratory of Ornithology) for their Northwest region, which includes Alberta, Saskatchewan, Montana, Idaho, and Wyoming. (For more on FeederWatch, please see Chapter 12.)

To cater to tastes as far apart as those of the Bohemian waxwing and Clark's nutcracker, it is necessary to provide a varied menu. Mrs. Eveland in Helena does this by providing halved apple for waxwings, and sunflower, canary seeds, suet, and suet-peanut butter mixes for her other birds. She makes waffles as a special treat for some of the birds. She says her birds won't eat corn, wheat, green apple, or whole wheat or brown bread. Perhaps they have been spoiled by all the other good food!

To provide something different for the birds, Ernie Kuyt in Edmonton ties together a bundle of grasses, millet, and sunflower heads and fastens it to a post. Like the sheath offered to birds at Christmastime in Scandinavia for centuries, it is a unique way of supplying food to birds without using a bird feeder.

Hummingbird Plants

The hummingbirds, so plentiful in most of the West, are largely absent on the open plains. But with the arrival of humans and changing habitats, the plains are becoming less forbidding for them. With the appearance of trees and gardens, hummingbirds can now find the food and shelter that was once lacking. This may help explain why so many western hummingbirds are expanding their ranges eastward and are appearing in fall and winter as far east as the northern coast of the Gulf of Mexico. Suitable garden flowers, along with sugar water feeders, help the hummingbirds reach their destinations and serve to encourage some of them to nest.

The same garden flowers I listed for the eastern Great Plains are well-suited as hummingbird plants in western portions as well. These include penstemon, cardinal flower, columbine, Indian paintbrush, and salvia. To these I can add a few others such as trumpet creeper, trumpet honeysuckle, bee balm, coralbells, larkspur, petunia, and scarlet runner bean.

Food Plants

Maples, ashes, and elms furnish winged seeds that provide an important food for many of the seed eaters, including the evening grosbeak, pine grosbeak, and the crossbills. Box elder, a maple often planted in shelter belts, is the tree that evening grosbeaks largely depend upon when they wander far out into the plains in fall and winter.

Mountain ash, grown widely as a street and yard tree, may lose its crop of red fruit clusters when robins, cedar and Bohemian waxwings pass through in the fall. Seeds not eaten in the fall will still be on the trees to supply much needed food for the birds when they return in spring. The same is true of pyracantha, whose bright red or orange fruit clusters are so decorative in fall and winter. Although primarily a plant of warmer regions, pyracantha can be grown as far north as Denver or farther if hardy varieties are used. Two of the best are the 'Lalandei' and 'Kasan' varieties of *Pyracantha coccinea*. For late summer and fall, Russian olive (*Elaeagnus angustifolia*) is one of the best bird food plants for this part of the West. It offers them heavy crops of reddish fruits. Drought-resistant and capable of withstanding almost any kind of weather, Russian olive is a perfect shrub for the yard, or for use in shelter belts.

For an ornamental, there is nothing that can equal the flowering crab apples. Showy blossoms in spring and brightly colored small apples attractive to birds in the fall make these shrubs or small trees ideal for yard plantings. One of the best for the plains region is hopa crab apple (*Malus floribunda*, var. 'Hopa'). Snowberry, with its white fruits, is a popular border plant that furnishes food for game birds and several of the finches. The cotoneasters are popular ornamentals that also have value as bird food plants. Several species can be grown as far north as the plains regions of Canada.

Special Problems

The Great Plains area, with its continental climate, can experience drastic changes in the weather during the colder months. Feeding birds when the weather is balmy one day and down to zero with gale force winds and blinding snow the next, calls for extra resourcefulness on our part. Using sturdy feeders and making the most of any shelter in the way of over-hanging eaves, a veranda, or the limbs of an evergreen can make for a savings in bird food and will offer better protection for our birds. A long trudge to reach bird feeders is dangerous in cold weather and should be avoided. Sometimes window feeders on the leeward side of the house are the answer. Remember, too, that water is still needed by birds in winter. This can be provided in a birdbath kept unfrozen with an electric heating element designed specifically for birdbaths.

While winter may seem dull and lifeless except for our bird feeders, we know that the cold weather will not last forever. When the sun comes out and the snow begins to melt, our efforts on behalf of birds are frequently rewarded. With spring's arrival there will be song in the air, and nesting activity will soon be getting underway. ☐

In winter, a simple heating device can keep water open for birds to bathe and drink.

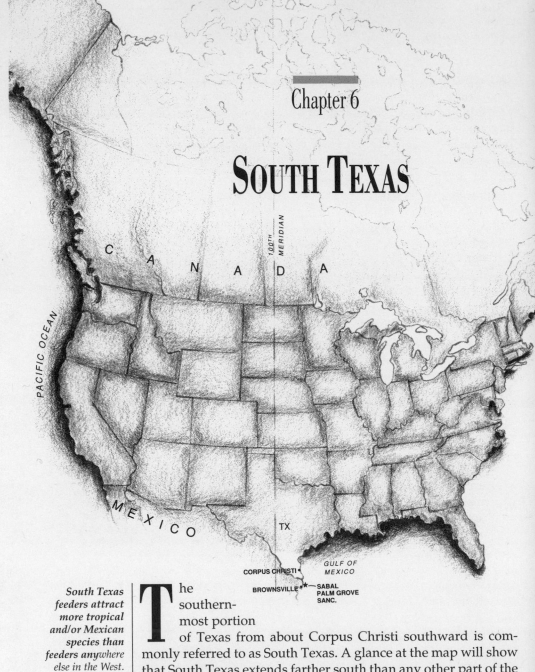

Chapter 6

SOUTH TEXAS

*South Texas
feeders attract
more tropical
and/or Mexican
species than
feeders anywhere
else in the West.*

The southern-most portion of Texas from about Corpus Christi southward is commonly referred to as South Texas. A glance at the map will show that South Texas extends farther south than any other part of the West. Brownsville, near the mouth of the Rio Grande, is less than 200 miles north of the Tropic of Cancer, which is regarded as the dividing line between tropic and temperate zones.

The birds we find here in South Texas seem to belong to the tropics rather than to our temperate zone. Here many western birds, from both sides of the border, obligingly appear east of the

100th meridian. Yet alongside such "exotic" birds as the chachalaca, white-tipped dove, green jay, and clay-colored robin will be widely familiar feeder birds such as the mourning dove, Carolina wren, and northern cardinal, and the ubiquitous European starling and house sparrow, which have followed human habitation expansion across North America. Downy and red-bellied woodpeckers are replaced in South Texas by ladder-backed and golden-fronted woodpeckers. The blue jay is replaced at many feeders by the brilliantly colored green jay. Chickadees and titmice are represented only by the black-crested race of the tufted titmouse. Resident olive and black-throated sparrows replace some of the northern sparrows that do not stray this far south in winter. Rounding out the list are several species of hummingbirds and orioles which visit feeders, proving beyond doubt that bird feeding in South Texas has many rewards.

Golden-fronted woodpeckers, common in South Texas, eat fruit, berries, insects, and some bird seeds.

Corpus Christi and Kingsville

As in so many other parts of North America, birds in South Texas are subject to shifts and changes in their ranges. This is best seen in pronounced northward range expansion in recent years by the black-bellied whistling duck, Inca dove, buff-bellied hummingbird, and great kiskadee. These four species, formerly regarded as residents of the extreme southern portion of Texas, are now being seen as far north as Beaumont and even southwestern Louisiana. Both the Inca dove and buff-bellied hummingbird are now common feeder birds throughout South Texas.

Corpus Christi, 150 miles north of the Rio Grande, is now well within the respective ranges of the white-tipped dove, green jay, and bronzed cowbird, all formerly regarded as birds of the Lower Rio Grande Valley.

For those who feed birds in towns and cities like Corpus Christi, Kingsville, and Falfurrias, there is the excitement of having both Lower Valley birds and passing migrants that follow the Texas Coast. The J. R. Swartzes in Corpus Christi see as many as five species of hummingbirds in their yard in the course of a year. Buff-bellied hummingbirds are present all year, the ruby-throated and black-chinned in spring and fall, the rufous in winter, and the broad-tailed in the fall. The latter two are far-western species that wander eastward to the Texas coast during the fall and winter. The Swartzes' yard also attracts Inca doves, long-billed thrashers, and bronzed cowbirds. They had their biggest thrill when, on February 22, 1987, lazuli buntings at their feeders were joined by several indigo buntings and a painted bunting! The Lower Rio Grande has two other buntings, of Mexican origin, that have appeared from time to time; the blue bunting is now appearing at a few bird feeders along the border, but so far the varied bunting has not. Perhaps someday a lucky feeding station operator in South Texas will report all five buntings at his or her feeder.

Jesse Grantham of Corpus Christi, besides having the same hummingbird species as the Swartzes, has more Inca doves than he would like. He says they chase other birds away, even mourning doves. Spring and fall migrants that appear at his feeders include indigo buntings, blue grosbeaks, dickcissels, Lincoln's sparrows, and occasionally, rose-breasted grosbeaks.

At Kingsville, about 25 miles closer to the Rio Grande Valley, Paul and Nancy Palmer have had as many as five different hummingbird species at their feeders in one day. Still other hummer species have appeared from time to time. Green jays are common at the Palmers' feeders, as are white-winged doves and curve-billed thrashers. A clay-colored robin, a rarity anywhere in South Texas, paid the Palmers a two-week visit one winter. Avian visitors from farther north include the red-winged blackbird and American goldfinch, and from farther west, the lesser goldfinch. Often there are more Inca doves and bronzed cowbirds than the Palmers would care to host. Seed-eating birds at the Palmers' feeders respond well to sunflower seeds and commercial mixes containing milo, canary seed, cracked corn, and other ingredients. Since the birds leave nothing untouched, the Palmers assume that everything in the mixture is popular.

The Lower Rio Grande Valley

Like oases amid the citrus groves and grain and cotton fields of South Texas, a series of refuges, parks, and nature preserves provide space where fast-vanishing native flora remains and birds abound. At many of these parks and wildlife refuges food and water are commonly provided for birds. At Sabal Palm Grove Sanctuary near Brownsville, the Santa Ana National Wildlife Refuge south of Alamo, and Bentsen-Rio Grande Valley State Park near Mission, visitors—with the help of bird feeders—can view some of the most exciting birds in South Texas at close quarters. Some of these birds are Mexican species whose ranges barely reach across the border. It is no wonder that every so often preserves such as Santa Ana furnish records of birds never before seen in the United States.

At Bentsen State Park dozens of campers living in recreation vehicles take advantage of excellent opportunities for viewing Mexican birds by luring them with food and water at their campsite feeding stations. Kay McCracken, author of *Birding South Texas*, describes the feeding which takes place:

"The pampered and spoiled golden-fronted woodpeckers, green jays, and Altamira orioles in the park prefer fruit provided by the campers to almost anything else. You see cut oranges sprouting on mesquite and hackberry trees all around the park."

In addition to fruit and more conventional bird foods, the campers serve a fair amount of what could be called "junk food." Clay-colored robins, recent arrivals from Mexico now breeding in South Texas, include popcorn and corn chips in their diets. The great kiskadee, a member of the flycatcher family, defies flycatcher tradition by eating suet. It also has the unflycatcher-like habit of plunging into water for small fish.

Bird feeders at Bentsen are also attended by plain chachalacas, white-tipped doves, mourning doves, ladder-backed woodpeckers, the black-crested race of the tufted titmouse, long-billed thrashers, bronzed cowbirds, cardinals, pyrrhuloxias, and olive sparrows.

Higher up on the Rio Grande, near the Falcon Dam is the town of Salineño, where equally exciting birds visit feeding stations, including brown jays, Audubon's and Altamira orioles.

In larger towns and cities, such as Harlingen and Brownsville, manicured lawns and exotic plants from the tropics replace the stands of native vegetation that are such a haven for birds.

Green jays (left, below) and Altamira orioles readily come to fruit.

Nevertheless, towns like McAllen, where I once fed birds, have resident Inca doves, white-winged doves, mourning doves, mockingbirds, cardinals, and within the last several years, escaped parrots and parakeets, which are easily adapting to the climate and living conditions of South Texas.

Both McAllen and Brownsville are home to sizable flocks of green parakeets and red-crowned parrots that travel widely throughout residential areas, occasionally visiting bird feeders. Although it is assumed that all of them either escaped into the wild or were released by their owners, it is possible that a few arrived from Mexico on their own. Several other members of the parrot family are also seen in the wild, including the black-hooded parakeet, yellow-headed, white-fronted, and lilac-crowned parrots, military macaw, and the budgerigar, a native of Australia.

At the southernmost tip of South Texas, only six miles southeast of Brownsville, is Sabal Palm Grove Sanctuary owned by the National Audubon Society. It was established primarily for the preservation of the rare Texas palm (*Sabal texana*), but it is also a mecca for birds. Birdbaths attract "fantastic numbers of birds during migration," according to Rose Farmer, the sanctuary manager. Besides some 20 species of migrant warblers, the baths have attracted strays from Mexico such as the golden-crowned warbler, gray-crowned yellowthroat, and a rare winter resident of the Lower Rio Grande Valley, the tropical parula.

As Rose Farmer indicates, water is largely responsible for bringing warblers and a number of rarities into close viewing range for the refuge's visitors. Like the Palmers in Kingsville, she offers birds a mixture of birdseeds, including sunflower, millet, and milo, and finds it is eagerly consumed. She supplements this food with finely cracked corn "because it is cheap and is readily available."

Both Palm Grove and Bentsen have had records of the crimson-collared grosbeak, a rarely encountered stray from Mexico. Many of the Lower Valley specialities seen at Bentsen and the Santa Ana Refuge, including chachalacas and olive sparrows, are also present at Palm Grove feeders. Needless to say, the rich bird life of South Texas makes bird feeding a popular and rewarding pastime.

More and More Hummingbirds

South Texas has only one resident hummingbird, the buff-bellied. It is an emerald green, with light buff below, a rufous

tail, and a red bill with a black tip. The sexes are alike in appearance, which is unusual in hummingbirds. In a range expansion beginning about 1960, the buff-bellied began moving northward from the Lower Rio Grande Valley. By the early 1970s, it had become established as a resident as far north as Corpus Christi and was beginning to appear in winter along the upper Texas coast and in southern Louisiana. As if this wasn't enough of a puzzle, during the same period several other species of western hummingbirds were being reported in fall and winter.

In *Birding South Texas*, Kay McCracken states that "Next to the rubythroat, the black-chinned is our most common hummer, since in our area their ranges overlap." She goes on to say, "Rufous hummers are regular here in winter. Less so are broadtailed, Allen's, and Anna's—though one winter we were invaded by Anna's. Buff-bellieds visit at any season and probably breed here." Kay reports rare visits by the green violet-ear, blue-throated, Costa's, and Lucifer hummingbirds. The green violet-ear is a Mexican species.

Why do so many hummingbirds congregate in winter in this part of coastal Texas and Louisiana? One can venture the guess that milder winters and bountiful nectar from plantings and hummingbird feeders have been factors in making it possible for the birds to survive. But this leaves unanswered the question of why so many far-western hummingbirds, including Costa's, Anna's, Allen's, Calliope, and rufous go all the way to the Texas Coast, 1,000 or more miles from their normal ranges.

During the warmer months there is no shortage of hummingbird flowers in Gulf Coast and South Texas gardens. Among the most attractive to hummingbirds are firecracker

Resident buff-bellied hummers respond well to sugar water feeders in South Texas.

plant (*Rusellia*), cape honeysuckle (*Tecomaria*), stonecrop (*Dudleya*), bottlebrush (*Callistemon*), coral bean (*Erythrina*), and citrus trees. There are also plants present that can survive desertlike conditions, including desert willow (*Chilopsis*), tree tobacco (*Nicotiana*), and flame flower (*Anisacanthus*). Red and orange blossoms seem to predominate in hummingbird gardens, but the birds also visit the white blossoms of citrus trees and the yellowish-green flowers of tree tobacco.

Food Plants for Other Birds

As in the eastern Great Plains, the hackberries, with their late summer and fall fruits, are excellent bird food plants. Two of the best are sugar hackberry (*Celtis laevigata*) and spiny hackberry (*Celtis pallida*). The latter is commonly known by the Spanish name granjeño. Equally popular with birds are anaqua (*Ehretia anacua*) and Chinese tallow tree (*Sapium sebiferum*). The tallow tree, from the Far East, is both colorful and useful since it bears capsules containing white, wax-coated seeds that birds readily consume in fall and winter.

Suitable for yard plantings are loquat, nandina, pyracantha, beautyberry (*Callicarpa*), and Barbados cherry. For those who like hot peppers and are willing to share them with birds, there is chilipiquin (*Capsicum annuum*).

Special Problems

In South Texas, as in so many other parts of North America, loss of natural habitat and damage to the environment is a serious problem. The small amount of unaltered habitat left for birds in this region is steadily diminishing. If it were not for protected lands and the green lawns and plantings of residential areas in towns and cities, much of the fascinating bird life of the region would have disappeared.

A much different problem is parasitism by cowbirds. This was a serious threat to songbirds when the brown-headed cowbird alone was laying its eggs in the nests of other birds. Recently it has been aggravated by the rapid increase of the bronzed cowbird, a species that has arrived from south of the border. Paul Palmer, whose bird feeders in Kingsville I reported upon earlier, states that both cowbird species have reached "plague levels" where he lives and are heavily parasitizing the nests of northern cardinals, green jays, hooded orioles, and probably Audubon's orioles. Smaller birds like vireos and warblers are particularly susceptible to nest losses from cowbirds.

Despite these problems South Texas still possesses a remarkable avifauna that thrives wherever the native plant life has been spared. With the help of bird feeders and birdbaths, many species that otherwise might escape notice can be watched at leisure. □

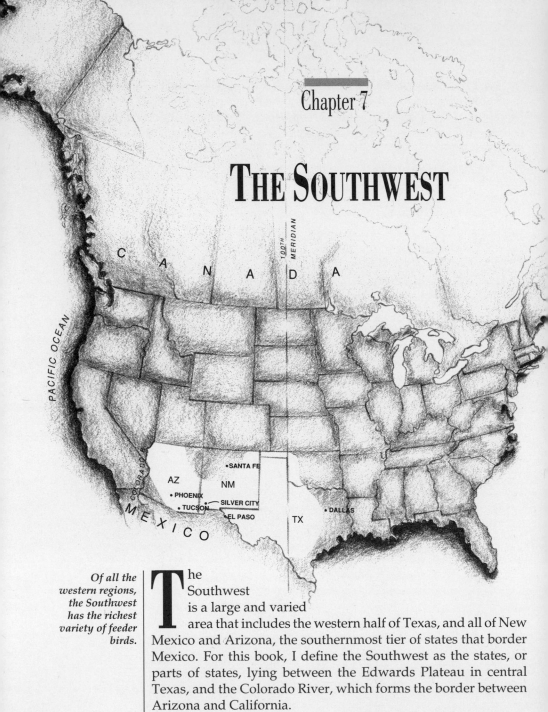

Chapter 7

THE SOUTHWEST

PACIFIC OCEAN

CANADA

100TH MERIDIAN

COLORADO R.

AZ

•SANTA FE

NM

•PHOENIX

SILVER CITY

•TUCSON

•EL PASO

•DALLAS

TX

MEXICO

Of all the western regions, the Southwest has the richest variety of feeder birds.

The Southwest is a large and varied area that includes the western half of Texas, and all of New Mexico and Arizona, the southernmost tier of states that border Mexico. For this book, I define the Southwest as the states, or parts of states, lying between the Edwards Plateau in central Texas, and the Colorado River, which forms the border between Arizona and California.

The Southwest has more bird species that visit feeders than any other part of the West. As in southern Texas, many of these species are Mexican birds whose ranges extend only a short distance north of the border.

Summer Flocks

Except in the mountains, where the landscape is forested, the southwestern countryside is largely open and birds easier to see. On a camping trip in the Southwest some years ago, I was struck by the fact that so many species remain gregarious during the height of the nesting season. I recall seeing flocks of birds wherever I went.

"The jays and their relatives," I wrote, "offered some of the best examples. In the Santa Rita Mountains of southern Arizona, I always found the gray-breasted jay in noisy flocks of from 15 to 25 individuals." The same was true of the pinyon jay, which frequents the juniper-pinyon forests in Utah. As the ornithologist William L. Finley reported, this species nests in colonies, and the birds remain in flocks throughout the nesting season. As I already knew, pinyon jays sometimes travel in enormous flocks during the winter. On the outskirts of Eagle Pass in Texas I saw 15 Chihuahuan (white-necked) ravens in one flock. Another example of a communally-oriented bird is the acorn woodpecker. In the Santa Rita Mountains there were always six to eight in the trees around my camping site.

My trip notes continued, "At the Grand Canyon in Arizona, I saw red crossbills, and in the mountains of Colorado, pine siskins in large flocks. I was surprised to see about 40 red crossbills at one time at an overlook where tourists view the Grand Canyon. The house finch is another bird I found in large numbers. On a barren hillside near Phoenix, I counted one flock of almost 100."

The presence of large flocks in summer explains why feeding stations in the Southwest can be inundated with birds at almost any time of year. Summer flocks are especially evident in higher mountain districts of the Southwest, where red crossbills, pine siskins, and many of the jays breed.

The greater roadrunner's diet includes insects, mammals, and reptiles. At feeders they eat meat scraps and hamburger.

Life Zones

One hundred years ago, the eminent naturalist Dr. C. Hart Merriam (the brother of Florence Merriam Bailey; see Chapter 1) devised a way of mapping the changes in vegetation, animal, and bird life that accompany changes in altitude in the western mountains. Using a mountain peak in Arizona as his model, Dr. Merriam delineated the zones based upon altitude and called them "life zones." He named them based upon the flora and fauna found in each.

In New Mexico and Arizona the climb starts with cactus and

desert birds, and with each zone certain bird species drop out and new ones take their place. At the highest levels, the avifauna resembles that which is found close to sea level in Washington or British Columbia. Nesting birds include the spruce grouse, white-crowned sparrow, red crossbill, pine grosbeak, and rosy finch!

Northward in Colorado, where the same zones occur at lower elevations, Alfred M. Bailey and Robert J. Niedrach, in their book *Birds of Colorado*, point out that the zonal concept is not as rigid as outlined by Dr. Merriam. They noted that horned larks breed in three zones in Colorado, and other species breed in one or more zones. But they add, "Each bird, generally speaking, has a certain habitat or type of environment within one zone where it may be expected to be more numerous than elsewhere at a given season."

Writing of western birds in the July/August 1989 issue of *Bird Watcher's Digest*, Roger Tory Peterson calls the life zones "convenient pigeonholes." In the same article, he captures the thrill of passing through several zones along a road in the western mountains:

"The landscape changes, the birds change, and so do we. There is a lift to the spirit in the sudden transition, heightened with each switch up the stony flanks of the mountain mass. . . There are places in the Southwest where we can go through five or six life zones in half a day, from desert lowlands similar to those of the hot, dry province of Sonora in Mexico, to the windswept spruce of the Hudsonian Zone, or even to draughty alpine meadows dotted with flowers that look just like those that carpet the subarctic tundra."

In New Mexico and Arizona, where some mountain peaks rise to 12,000 or 13,000 feet, five life zones are recognized. Knowing these zones and the birds to expect in them is a useful guide to those who feed birds. The chart below lists the life zones and their elevations in New Mexico as given by J. Stokely Ligon in his book *New Mexico Birds*. Under the zone headings I list a few of the characteristic nesting birds found in each. The life zone concept is applicable throughout the West wherever altitude changes cause changes in habitat types.

Lower Sonoran Zone (2,850 to 4,200 feet)

Gambel's quail, Costa's hummingbird, cactus wren, verdin, blue grosbeak, summer tanager.

Upper Sonoran Zone (4,200 to 7,400 feet)

Broad-tailed and black-chinned hummingbirds, hairy wood-pecker, scrub and gray-breasted jays, plain titmouse, mountain chickadee, hepatic tanager, canyon towhee, yellow-eyed junco (in S. E. Arizona).

Transition Zone (7,400 to 8,500 feet)

Steller's jay, red-breasted nuthatch, western bluebird, western tanager, evening grosbeak.

Canadian Zone (8,500 to 11,500 feet)

Green-tailed towhee, pine grosbeak, Cassin's finch, horned lark.

Hudsonian Zone (11,500 to 13,000 feet)

White-crowned sparrow, rosy finch, horned lark.

Seasonal Movements

After the nesting season, many species of the higher elevations will descend to lower elevations. This is true of both migrants and residents. A few species actually ascend to higher levels for a brief time after the nesting season to take advantage of natural food supplies. Among the birds apt to do so are the American robin, mountain bluebird, and black-headed grosbeak. As a rule, mountain species that do not undertake long migrations remain in the mountains until snow and cold force them to descend to the foothills and plains. But some birds are little daunted by bad weather. The rosy finches are so well adapted to wintry conditions that only the heaviest snows and bitter cold will cause them to leave the high mountain peaks where they make their home. As soon as the weather amelio-

Thick scrub habitat of the Southwest is home to the pyrrhuloxia. Below, at left, is the male.

*Inca doves
are common at
feeders in the
Southwest,
particularly in
towns and cities.*

rates, they return to the mountains.

For those who feed birds at lower elevations, the uncertainties can make for an exciting season since there is no way of knowing what the winter will bring. If it brings mountain birds, there may be questions about their identification, as well as feeding habits. How they will interact with other birds already at the feeding station? Some of the information on feeding Rocky Mountains birds provided in Chapter 8 may be helpful when these invasions occur.

Central Texas

There is a gradual transition from eastern to western birds in this region. Those who live to the east of the Edwards Plateau in San Antonio, Austin, Dallas, and Fort Worth can expect only a few truly western birds at their feeders. Barbara Ramming, who lives in a suburb of Dallas, has only two western species that visit her feeders: black-chinned hummingbird and rufous-crowned sparrow. A few more western birds appear on the home grounds of Hans J. Mueller, who maintains feeders at Wimberly, about 30 miles north of San Antonio. Among them are the Inca dove, greater roadrunner, black-chinned hummingbird, ladder-backed woodpecker, and scrub jay. Moreover, he has such wide-ranging birds at his feeders as Bewick's wren, northern cardinal, blue grosbeak, painted bunting, and house finch— none of which can be classified as distinctly eastern or western.

Much the same can be reported for the birds at Betty and Dan Baker's feeding station in Bulverde, Texas to the north of San Antonio, within the eastern fringes of the Edwards Plateau. They have several of the same species listed by Mr. Mueller and also the golden-fronted woodpecker, which ranges from south-central Oklahoma southward. During most winters, they have pine siskins, American goldfinches, and chipping sparrows, and as a year-round resident, the black-crested race of the tufted titmouse.

Westward, within the Edwards Plateau, the juniper-clad slopes provide breeding grounds for many species. Here, where the 100th meridian cuts across the center of the plateau, more western birds make their appearance. The northern bobwhite is replaced by the scaled quail, the red-bellied woodpecker by the golden-fronted, and the Carolina wren by the rock wren and canyon wren. In the wooded river bottoms of the area many eastern species reach the western limits of their ranges.

Farther west, on the plains of western Texas, the countryside becomes drier and more open. Towns are farther apart, and the dim outlines of mountain peaks can be seen far in the distance.

West Texas

El Paso, at an elevation of 3,760 feet, is within the lower limits of the Upper Sonoran Zone. Here, at the extreme southwestern corner of Texas, more than half the feeder birds will be distinctly western while most of the others will be wide-ranging species like the mourning dove and red-winged blackbird. This mix is reflected in the birds reported by Barry R. Zimmer at his El Paso feeders. His sugar water feeders are visited by five species of hummingbirds and the northern (Bullock's) oriole. Sunflower seed and mixed birdseeds attract the Inca dove, scrub jay, great-tailed grackle, pyrrhuloxia, Cassin's finch, green-tailed towhee, canyon (brown) towhee, lesser goldfinch, Brewer's sparrow, lark bunting, and black-throated sparrow, all distinctly western birds.

Southwestern New Mexico

For feeder birds at a somewhat higher elevation to the west near Silver City, New Mexico, I have been supplied with a long list by Ralph A. Fisher, Jr. Beginning in April, his hummingbird feeders are visited by black-chinned hummingbirds. By late August, when the hummers leave, he may have had five or six other individual hummers competing for a place at his two hummingbird feeders with northern, Scott's, and hooded orioles. A magnificent hummingbird, a rarity in his region, appeared during the summer of 1989. Sugar water has also attracted the northern mockingbird, summer tanager, and house finch to his feeders.

Many of Mr. Fisher's bird visitors feed on the ground where a plentiful supply of milo brings in mourning doves, whitewinged doves, Gambel's quail, and a special visitor, the Montezuma quail, which seldom comes out into the open where it can be seen. The milo is also favored by other birds, including house finch, green-tailed, rufous-sided (spotted) and canyon towhees, as well as juncos and a number of sparrow species. Apple halves impaled on a post top attract two close relatives, the northern cardinal and pyrrhuloxia, and several other birds that seem to need a thirst-quenching fruit when it is dry. To cater to woodpeckers, jays, mountain chickadees, plain titmice, and white-breasted nuthatches that appear in winter, Mr. Fisher supplies generous amounts of suet. No doubt the varied food offerings are the primary reason so many birds visit his yard.

At an elevation of 4,800 feet, Mr. Fisher's yard is well within the limits of the Upper Sonoran Zone. He can expect mountain birds in winter, migrants that pass through each season, and resident species. His location is an enviable one for bird feeding.

Southeastern Arizona

At about the same elevation but to the southwest at the foot of the Chiricahua Mountains in southeastern Arizona, Sally and Walter Spofford maintain a bird feeding operation similar to Mr. Fisher's, attracting many of the same species. When they began feeding birds at their home at the edge of the small community of Portal, they discovered that their location was an ideal one for hummingbirds. Only 40 miles north of the Mexican border, they were in a part of Arizona that plays host to "just-across-the-border species" and others that range more widely in this country. (Border species occur all along the Rio Grande in Texas and in the southernmost portions of New Mexico, Arizona, and California.)

The Spoffords have the philosophy that all wildlife that comes their way is welcome and entitled to the food and water they offer. This includes raccoons, foxes, ring-tailed cats, coatis, and bats, which are nocturnal visitors and are attracted by sugar water in easy-to-drink-from cups. Diurnal guests include as many as 12 species of hummingbirds each year. As so many others have discovered, birds other than hummingbirds are fond of sugar water and will drink their share at hanging feeders. To make it easier for these tipplers, the Spoffords have provided sugar water in the same open cups that mammal visitors drink from at night. Over the years, they have observed no fewer than 19 bird species, other than hummingbirds, drinking sugar water. This is an amazing record that few other feeding stations could duplicate.

Besides sugar water, the Spoffords' guests have a choice of at least ten other foods. The most popular ones are black oil sunflower, milo, and a homemade suet cake mixture. The least popular food is millet. For harder-to-attract species, the Spoffords will offer something special. For example, greater roadrunners come to the windowsill to receive pieces of raw beef, and bridled titmice, curve-billed thrashers, and canyon wrens have special places where they can find mealworms. Extra attentions, such as these, have helped boost the number of species recorded over the years at the feeders to an impressive total of 64!

As with Mr. Fisher, who has had an equally large number of species coming to his feeders, location plays an important part in the Spoffords' success. Amid a background of lofty peaks, at the mouth of a canyon with a stream, they enjoy a part of Arizona that is not only a mecca for birds but one of the most scenic in the state.

Tucson and Nearby Mountains

One hundred miles to the west is Tucson, at an elevation of 2,400 feet, having birds typical of the Lower Sonoran Zone. Thanks to the presence of water, food at feeding stations, and plantings, the bird population in residential sections of Tucson greatly exceeds that of the outlying desert scrubland. According to J. T. Emlen, in a 1974 issue of *The Condor*, the bird population density is 26 times that of what it was before humans changed the landscape. Seed-eating birds have benefited the most. They have a ready supply of seeds from weeds, lawn grasses, and seeds and grain supplied at bird feeders. Trees and shrubs in the city supply both fruits and insects that feed on vegetation. All of the birds benefit greatly from the water brought in for human consumption and agricultural irrigation.

William Davis, a retired physician, who is an authority on Arizona birds, offers milo, millet, wheat, and cracked corn to birds in his yard and also sugar water for hummingbirds. The birds he attracts are much the same as those that visit feeders in other parts of Tucson. Standard birds, as he calls them, are Gambel's quail, white-winged, mourning, and Inca doves, curve-billed thrashers, cactus wrens, northern cardinals, pyr-rhuloxias, house sparrows, house finches, canyon towhees, and in winter, white-crowned sparrows. He calls the house finch the most abundant bird in Tucson, while bronzed and brown-headed cowbirds are occasional visitors.

His hummingbird feeders are patronized by the black-chinned hummingbird in summer and by the Anna's in winter. Other sugar water patrons include Gila woodpecker, verdin, house finch, and hooded oriole. A neighbor has had an orange-crowned warbler at his hummingbird feeder during winter.

Dr. Davis' most unusual feeding station visitor was a western screech-owl. During rehabilitation from an injury, the owl had been fed cat food by Dr. Davis. Once released it continued to come for the same food placed outside, and later brought its mate and several offspring.

Water at birdbaths is inviting to all of the birds that come to his feeders, and also to a nonfeeder bird, the phainopepla, a member of the silky-flycatcher family. The phainopepla is a typical Lower Sonoran bird that feeds mainly upon mistletoe berries, insects, and other small fruits. It is one of the desert birds that has adapted to the lusher vegetation of the suburbs of the Southwest.

To the west of Tucson is the Arizona-Sonora Desert Museum with exhibitions of the flora and fauna of the surrounding desert. Feeders and water sources at the museum are patronized by Gambel's quail, cactus wrens, northern cardinals, pyrrhuloxias, house finches, and canyon towhees.

In the mountains surrounding Tucson are the upper limits of the Upper Sonoran Zone; here conditions are much the same as in Portal, where the Spoffords live. Oaks, pinyon pine, and juniper replace the cactus, catclaw, and mesquite. Many more kinds of hummingbirds are present and there is a greater diversity in the bird life in general. All of this can be enjoyed to full advantage at Madera Canyon in the Santa Rita Mountains to the south of Tucson, within the Coronado National Forest. Here, at the Santa Rita Lodge, is another of the area's premier feeding operations.

Special birds of the area found at the lodge's seed and grain feeders will be the acorn woodpecker, Strickland's woodpecker, bridled titmouse, blue grosbeak, and yellow-eyed (Mexican) junco. The hummer feeders are often crowded with as many as 12 hummingbird species, busily feeding at one time. In total 15 hummingbird species have been recorded here. Black-chinned and broad-billed hummingbirds are the most common species in summer, followed by the magnificent hummingbird. The list of likely hummers includes Anna's, Costa's, Lucifer, Calliope, and, irregularly, white-eared hummingbird, berylline hummingbird, and plain-capped starthroat. The hummingbird feeders also lure painted redstarts and Scott's orioles in to drink.

Margaret Loges, who lives at Oracle in Arizona, supplies sunflower, corn, and suet at her feeders, and has many of the birds that one would expect in the Upper Sonoran Zone to the south. The Inca dove, Gila woodpecker, curve-billed thrasher, house finch, and pyrrhuloxia all are regular visitors. In her yard, she notes that Gambel's quail and cactus wrens take dust baths, rather than water baths.

Hummingbird Plants

During the course of their evolution, plants that require hummingbirds as their pollinators have developed the enticements that ensure success. A bright color, a plentiful supply of nectar, and floral structures that will suit hummingbirds and keep out others are the main characteristics of hummingbird flowers. Hummingbird flowers are apt to be scentless, as fragrance would attract such competitors as bees and butterflies.

Curve-billed thrashers and many other species will eat watermelon at a feeder.

Nowhere are these flowers more abundant than in the Sonoran zone of the Southwest, where they support the region's many hummingbird species. Many hummingbird-specific plants are naturally timed so their spring bloomings match the appearance of the hummingbirds that will pollinate them. Some of these ornithophilous flowers, as they are called, are so specialized that their blossoms are shaped to fit the bills of the hummingbird species that act as their pollinators.

In its winter newsletter of 1989, the Arizona-Sonora Desert Museum lists 54 different hummingbird plants native to the region, giving their floral colors and flowering seasons. For any who doubt the importance of red in bringing hummingbirds to bird feeders, it is significant that slightly over 75 percent of the flowers are red, in some cases producing both red and orange, or red and yellow flowers. Red, however, was not the only enticing color. The remaining flowers are divided about equally between pink, orange, and yellow.

Some of the flowers produce blossoms throughout the years. This is true of chuparosa (*Justicia californica*), powder puff (*Calliandra californica*), and tree tobacco (*Nicotiana glauca*). Several others, including yellow elder (*Tecoma stans*), monkey-flowers (*Mimulus*), and autumn sage (*Salvia greggi*), bloom from early spring until the end of summer or later. This is also true of bleeding heart, a well-known garden flower suitable for some parts of the Southwest.

Other flowers, with shorter blooming seasons, that are popular with hummingbirds include the penstemons and Indian paintbrush (*Castilleja coccinea*) which are at their best in the spring. Coralbells (*Heuchera sanguinea*) blossoms through the spring and early summer. Trumpet creeper (*Campsis radicans)*) shows its blossoms during the summer and fall. For winter, there is the fuchsia-flowered gooseberry (*Ribes speciosum*).

For those who have property containing desert flora, there are the agave or century plants, claret-cup cactus (*Echinocereus*), and ocotillo with its spring blossoms. Even though the Southwest has a spectacular variety of hummingbird plants, there can be long periods of drought when few blossoms are available. Together with introduced garden flowers and sugar water feeders, plantings of hummingbird flowers can be life savers for hummingbirds. □

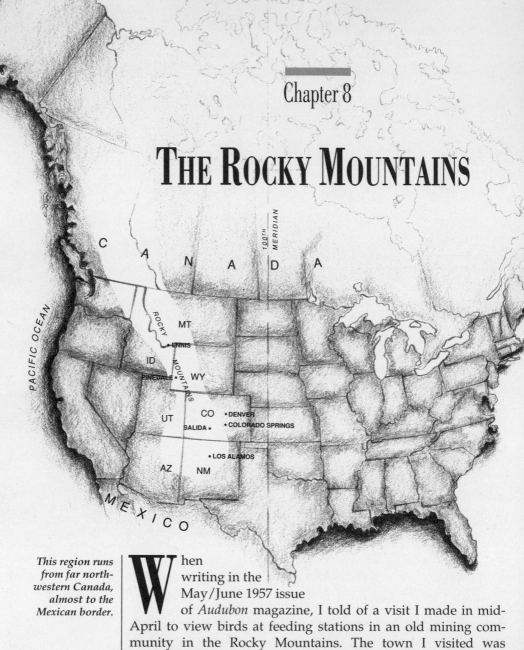

Chapter 8

THE ROCKY MOUNTAINS

This region runs from far north-western Canada, almost to the Mexican border.

When writing in the May/June 1957 issue of *Audubon* magazine, I told of a visit I made in mid-April to view birds at feeding stations in an old mining community in the Rocky Mountains. The town I visited was Georgetown, Colorado, at an elevation of 8,500 feet, about 70 miles west of Denver. I had heard that about half the people in this community, which presently has a population of 850, feed birds. I especially wanted to see rosy finches.

High mountain birds, the rosy finches are so well adapted to the harsh conditions that exist above the timberline that they come down to lower elevations only during the winter. And even then they retreat to the mountains again when conditions allow.

For several years Georgetown had had semi-permanent winter flocks that were composed of three distinctive races—the brown-capped being the most common, followed by the gray-crowned and the black rosy finch, a rarity. True to their nature, they appeared at feeders only when snow was on the ground and temperatures were colder than normal. In their habits and behavior the three races were indistinguishable. The birds I observed would spend much of their time in treetops, and as if given a signal, would drop down to the several yards where food was offered to them. Feeding for a while, mostly on the ground, they would leave as suddenly as they came.

Feeding stations had brought many other kinds of birds to Georgetown as well. The busiest and most noisy visitors were the Steller's jays. It was hard to believe that any bird could be so blue and beautiful and have such a roguish disposition. The bird's long pointed crest and harlequinlike facial stripes were in keeping with its bold and playful manner. Whenever one of the jays spotted a cat or a bird it disliked, it would set up a noisy chatter that was taken up by all the jays in the vicinity. Shouting insults, or so it seemed to my ear, the birds would move from tree to tree in a high state of excitement as they followed the object of their indignation. But when approaching a feeding station, the birds would become quiet, almost stealthy. At one yard, the jays would arrive one at a time and usually each would take a spin on a revolving clothesline before dropping down to eat. Propelled by the wind, the hanger, with its passenger, would revolve a number of times, giving the bird a merry ride.

The Clark's nutcracker, more crowlike than jaylike, was another of the town's wilderness birds that had succumbed to the temptation of unlimited food supplies. More confiding than the jays, which never lost a certain wariness, the nutcrackers would keep right on eating when people passed close by. Meatbirds, as they are sometimes called, they showed their preference for meat by feeding exclusively at suet feeders, ignoring grain. One resident told me that when he caught a mouse and threw it out on the snow a nutcracker would arrive and carry it away. If suet wasn't securely wedged into a holder, it would also be carried away. With their powerful bills, they were capable of breaking the wire mesh that held the suet. The nutcrackers and jays tilted their heads back when swallowing food. This, I decided, was to get an assist from gravity in helping the food go down.

Rosy finches are residents of the Rockies. Some winters they inundate lowland feeders.

Both the mountain and black-capped chickadees were common visitors at the Colorado feeders. The two would feed together without any show of antagonism. Sleeker and more tidy looking, to my eyes, the black-capped was just as much at home high in the Rockies as it is anywhere else. The mountain chickadee, with its contrasting facial pattern of black and white, seemed to wear a never-ending quizzical expression. Both species were equally tame and easily taught to feed from the hand.

Of the juncos that thronged about areas where birds were fed, the slate-colored (now considered a race of the dark-eyed junco) was the plainest looking of the four kinds present. The Oregon and gray-headed races, along with a few wintering white-winged juncos, were better marked and easy to recognize. They did much of their feeding in depressions in the snow where windblown seeds and grain from feeders had lodged. Here, out of the wind and sheltered from the cold, they ate in comfort. The American tree sparrow, another small bird well-adapted to the cold, also did most of its feeding on the ground. Downy and hairy woodpeckers at the suet feeders seemed oblivious to the cold. The same was true of white and red-breasted nuthatches. Red-naped sapsuckers, flickers, and Lewis' woodpeckers, I was told, were much more likely to come in the fall.

If I strolled any distance from the town, the bird life all but disappeared, except for the American dipper in rushing mountain streams and an occasional magpie, gray jay, or Townsend's solitaire. This is a common experience in the winter woods. Birds are often found where the people (and reliable food supplies) are.

The bird life at feeding stations in the Rocky Mountains region changes greatly in summer. Black-headed grosbeaks and western tanagers visit feeders and bring their young. Green-tailed towhees, unlike the timid rufous-sided towhee, are a dominant bird at feeders in summer, almost tame enough to take food from the hand. Hummingbirds are present in good numbers. The broad-tailed hummingbird is a summer resident and the rufous hummingbird, which migrates northward by way of the Pacific coastal region, appears in July and August on its return flight through the Rockies. Southbound rufous hummers reach Colorado at the end of June!

When I returned to Georgetown one year in early June, I tried a simple experiment with the broad-tailed hummingbirds. I was told that when they arrived in spring, they always returned to the exact spot where a feeder had hung the year before, a behavior which has been observed in other hummingbird species as well. It is a signal for people to put up their hummingbird feeders if they haven't already done so. With the permission of a homeowner, I tried moving the feeder that the hummers were used to, to the other side of the house. Within an hour the birds had discovered their old feeder at its new location.

At any season, bird feeding in Georgetown is highly productive. More than 57 species have been recorded at the feeders. Some were present every year in good numbers; others, like the rose-breasted grosbeak, lazuli bunting, and Harris' sparrow, are vagrants that might appear once and not come back again. The house sparrow, once common, is now scarce in this area, and there had been few occurrences of common grackles and brown-headed cowbirds and none of starlings. No one complained about this!

The bird life I had seen in this part of the Rockies closely resembles that of the mountainous regions southward into northern Arizona and New Mexico, and northward into Canada. The same birds are found at higher elevations to the south and at lower elevations to the north. Whether the spot was an old mining town, like Georgetown, a picnic area, a campground, a ski slope, or a vacation cabin in the Rockies, the birds would be there if given any encouragement at all in the form of food and water.

Northern Arizona

At Flagstaff, a little more than 200 miles north of Tucson, the elevation is higher (6,900 feet) and the climate is much cooler. Here, mountain birds have taken the place of desert birds. Instead of 15 species of hummingbirds, as in southeastern Arizona,

Steller's jays can be very aggressive at feeders, scaring away all other birds for a time.

only three are likely visitors to feeders in this region. The broad-tailed and black-chinned nest, and the rufous passes through during its July-to-October flight southward.

A number of species, including the Lewis' woodpecker, pinyon jay, Cassin's finch, and pine grosbeak, are at the southern limits of their ranges in this part of Arizona. Evening and pine grosbeaks, which nest at higher elevations, often appear in Flagstaff in winter. Another high elevation nester, the green-tailed towhee, stops by during spring and fall migration periods.

Living at the foot of a wooded mesa at the edge of town, Judith Fishback couldn't be better situated for supplying food and water to birds. Instead of Gila woodpeckers, she has quarrelsome Lewis' woodpeckers, which nest nearby and chase away nearly all her feeder birds in late May and early June. This is when the Lewis' are busiest with their nesting duties and are very territorial. Peaceful acorn woodpeckers visit her feeders for sunflower seed, and every once in a while, a northern flicker will settle down at the feeder and defend it—even from the powerful attack of the Lewis' woodpecker.

Although her feeders are highly popular with the birds, Ms. Fishback finds that water is by far her best drawing card. After substituting a homemade rock basin as a birdbath (replacing a galvanized garbage can lid) she began having more birds than she could always identify! She had no trouble with such unusual species as the blue grosbeak, rose-breasted grosbeak, and hepatic tanager when they appeared. But one day in late May a parakeetlike bird appeared, and its identity completely baffled her. It joined the last of her wintering evening grosbeaks, appearing daily at the bath and bird feeder. She eventually learned that it was a Fischer's lovebird from Tanzania, an escaped cage bird. It visited her yard all summer and left with a flock of black-headed grosbeaks in early fall.

Ms. Fishback finds that water is most popular with birds during the late spring/early summer dry period. Once wet weather sets in, the bath loses its appeal as the birds take advantage of numerous natural water sources. Robins continue to splash in her birdbath year-round, but in winter, many species prefer snow to water for drinking purposes.

Northern New Mexico

The bird life of north-central New Mexico is very similar to that of northern Arizona, despite the differences in life zones between the two regions. At about 7,500 feet, Helen Keller, Jo

Hall, and Lois Simpson, who feed birds in Santa Fe, are in the Transition Zone. Their feeders are visited in winter by pinyon jays, mountain chickadees, bushtits, Cassin's finches, and pine and evening grosbeaks. Present the entire year are plain titmice, house finches, pine siskins, and rufous-sided and canyon towhees. Summer feeder visitors include mourning dove, western tanager, and black-headed grosbeak.

Natalie Owens, who lives in ranching country to the northwest of Santa Fe, is about 1,000 feet lower in elevation. Well within the Upper Sonoran Zone, she has a somewhat different clientele at her feeders, including magpies, crows, ravens, and other birds. Using dog food pellets for the larger birds, and seed mixtures, fruit, and suet cakes for smaller ones, she manages to provide food for all her visitors without causing undue competition. She sometimes offers these birds a doughlike ball made of yellow cornmeal, bread, and peanut butter to which safflower oil has been added.

Ms. Owens reports that nearly all the birds visiting her yard eat the "olives" of the Russian olive. They digest only the fleshy portion of these fruits, discarding the pits in their droppings, and perhaps helping to spread this plant to new localities.

Northern Idaho/Eastern Washington

On the edge of the northern Rockies at Hayden Lake in northwestern Idaho, Mrs. Kenneth Hughes has an interesting variety of bird species coming to her feeders. Her location places her at the convergence of three distinctive regions, the Rocky Mountains, the Pacific Northwest, and the Great Basin. Among the species she attracts are the chestnut-backed chickadee, red-breasted nuthatch, American robin, Swainson's thrush, purple finch, and, with the help of peanut butter, brown creeper, golden-crowned kinglet, and MacGillivray's warbler. Her varied menu includes sunflower seeds, mixed birdseeds, cracked corn, niger, popcorn, and sugar water. For a period of about three weeks in late summer, the Calliope, rufous, and black-chinned hummingbirds at her feeders consume up to six quarts of sugar water per day!

Food for Rocky Mountain Birds

As in the western Great Plains, sunflower seed is the most popular food used by my correspondents at their feeding stations in the Rockies. Although nearly everyone uses sunflower in the shell, unshelled nut meats packaged by many of the suppliers of birdseeds are becoming more popular. For example, Barbara Wise of Pinedale, Wyoming, says that she buys primarily sunflower meats.

"They are more economical," she writes. "The birds are saved time and energy, and the discarded shells don't pile up."

Mixed birdseeds were second in popularity. The millets, which constitute such a large part of the mixtures, are sometimes offered separately. White proso millet is recommended over red millet. Cracked corn, another common ingredient, is poorly rated except as a food for the Steller's jay. Niger or thistle seed is not widely used, and is primarily regarded as a food for pine siskins. Suet and suet mixes, as might be expected where the winters are cold, are widely used and have many takers among the mountain birds. Beef kidney suet is recommended over other kinds.

To help birds caught in a sudden spring snowstorm, Barbara Wise offers emergency foods that are appealing to robins, bluebirds, warblers, and even an occasional flycatcher. Among the foods she uses are grated cheese, cottage cheese, ground dried fruits, cornbread, and grated suet. She points out that many people use dry dog and cat foods in bird feeding, and recommends that during emergencies these foods should be crumbled, not crushed. Kitten and puppy foods serve better for this purpose than adult pet foods. So that birds will see and utilize foods of this kind, she suggests that they be placed on packed snow or a driveway. The owners' pets should not be turned loose at such times!

Clark's nutcrackers are very fond of suet.

Water

Despite the advice I have given about supplying water to birds in winter for drinking and bathing, observations from the

Rockies suggest that water at this season may not have to be
supplied. Clinton Abbott writes in a 1929 issue of *The Condor* that
Steller's jays being fed in winter at a mountain resort hotel in
Colorado didn't take advantage of water supplied for them. He
stated that they prefer snow and that they "guzzle snow billful
after billful." They also pounded off pieces of icicles and ate them.

Barbara Wise in Pinedale, Wyoming, also downplays the
importance of water in winter. She writes: "Surprisingly, the
finches (who like salt) are about the only birds that use water we
provide in winter. Thaw areas, melt at rooflines, puddles, and
the edges of streams are used for drinking and bathing. Many
birds have learned to perch and drink on the edges of large,
heated tanks for cows and horses." But to the south in the
mountains of Arizona, Judith Fishback offers somewhat different evidence. She writes: "Since it is very dry here, I have a hard
time keeping water out for the birds. At dawn when I get up they
are lined up staring at the ice by the dozens." Since most of her
birds were house finches, this statement actually isn't very much
at odds with what Barbara Wise had to say.

Judith Fishback, whose birdbaths have attracted more than
30 species, reports that water was most popular in May and June,
the driest time of the year. After the rains come later in the
summer, only the robins pay much attention to the baths. "They
bathe religiously at dawn and dusk. When the fledglings are out
of the nest, they all try to bathe at one time. A strain on the fa-
cilities!" she states.

Patricia R. Snider, who lives in the southern Rockies near
Los Alamos, New Mexico, credits water with attracting a number of species that do not come to her bird feeders. These include
the robin, western bluebird, western tanager, and several warblers. Another hard-to-attract species, the lesser goldfinch readily comes to water in the Rockies and elsewhere in the West. Like
many of the other finches, it must drink frequently to help digest
the seeds it eats.

Feeding Hummingbirds

The Rockies are not home to as many hummingbird species
as are the mountains of southern Arizona and New Mexico.
Nevertheless, the region does have four common species that
can be depended upon and a number of others that appear from
time to time. From northern Wyoming southward, the broad-
tailed is the common nesting species. Their return flight southward is largely made by way of mountain peaks above timber-

line. The Calliope, the smallest of our hummers, ranges south-ward from British Columbia through the western Rockies to Utah. The rufous, the most northerly breeding of our hummingbirds, ranges in the Rockies from Alaska to western Montana. Like the two previous species, its return flight is by way of high mountain ridges. The black-chinned hummingbird, one of our most common species in the West, includes both mountains and lower elevations in its broad range, but does not ascend as high as the other three species.

This rough outline of ranges should not be interpreted too strictly. Hummingbirds have a tendency to wander. This explains why Barbara Wise, who lives at Pinedale, Wyoming, at an altitude of 7,200 feet, normally has all four species at her feeders in late summer. The many western hummingbirds that appear in the fall as far east as the coasts of Texas and Louisiana are another example of the wandering tendencies of these small birds.

Plants to entice hummingbirds in the Rockies should be ones able to withstand wide variations in the climate. Some of the best for this region are garden sage (*Salvia officinalis*), paintbrush, columbine, larkspur, cardinal flower, bee balm (*Monarda*), coralbells, lupine, and penstemon.

Rich Anderson, who feeds birds at Salida, Colorado, at an elevation of 8,800 feet, offers good advice on when to stop feeding hummingbirds. He says that people take down their hummingbird feeders in his part of Colorado on Labor Day because they think that the continued presence of food will cause the hummers to delay their migration south. He emphatically states that this simply is not true. Hummingbirds are hardy enough to withstand below freezing temperatures when they arrive in Colorado in late April; therefore, the somewhat milder average temperatures in September would not impose any hardship on them. Furthermore, presence of food at feeders will not prevent hummingbirds from migrating. As with other migrants, they leave when their inner promptings tell them to do so. In light of these facts, Mr. Anderson does not close down his hummingbird feeding operation until well after the last bird has departed.

Special Problems

Nearly everywhere small mammals take advantage of bird feeding stations to secure food for themselves. In parts of the Rockies, large mammals, like deer, moose, and sometimes even black bear, arrive and create unexpected problems. Barbara Wise says that moose are common visitors to her backyard. "They are especially demanding regarding handouts and will look in windows and follow people up on the deck or porch. They know where the bird feeders are and will often knock them down trying to get at the food." She says they especially like corn and sunflower seed. As if this were not enough of a problem, the moose, as well as deer, browse upon the plantings she has in her yard. "Gardening is difficult enough in the high Rockies," she states, "without gnawing and browsing by mammals." But she takes these problems philosophically and offers good advice on how mammal feeding should be conducted. At designated places proper types of food should be offered to mammals so that "when unusual or devastating weather occurs, there is an increased chance the animals will survive."

In regard to what to feed deer and moose, she states that hay can be harmful to deer but is more easily digested by moose. Both can be given alfalfa pellets, cracked corn, and millet. Salt blocks should be provided for both birds and mammals. She has seen finches pecking at salt crystals that had formed on tree stumps where salt blocks had been placed.

Reports from other parts of the Rockies indicate that both white-tailed and mule deer present problems to those who feed birds. A correspondent from Ennis, Montana, complained that the deer sometimes cleaned out the bird feeders in one night. Compared to large mammals, the smaller ones, such as squirrels, seemed relatively harmless, and many feeder operators were only too pleased to have them.

As an example of the mammals to expect on lower slopes of the Rockies near Colorado Springs, Katherine F. Spahn has black-phased, tassel-eared squirrels coming to her bird feeders along with fox squirrels, chipmunks, and rock squirrels. The chipmunks, according to Ms. Spahn, eat fallen niger seeds. She has no complaints about any of her feeder visitors.

Golden-mantled ground squirrels, present at nearly every picnic area and campground in the Rockies, also appear at bird feeders. When winter comes, the small mammals are much less in evidence. Many of them are in their burrows spending the winter hibernating in a semi-dormant state. □

Rocky mountain feeding stations can sometimes have a big mammal problem, since even moose will visit feeders!

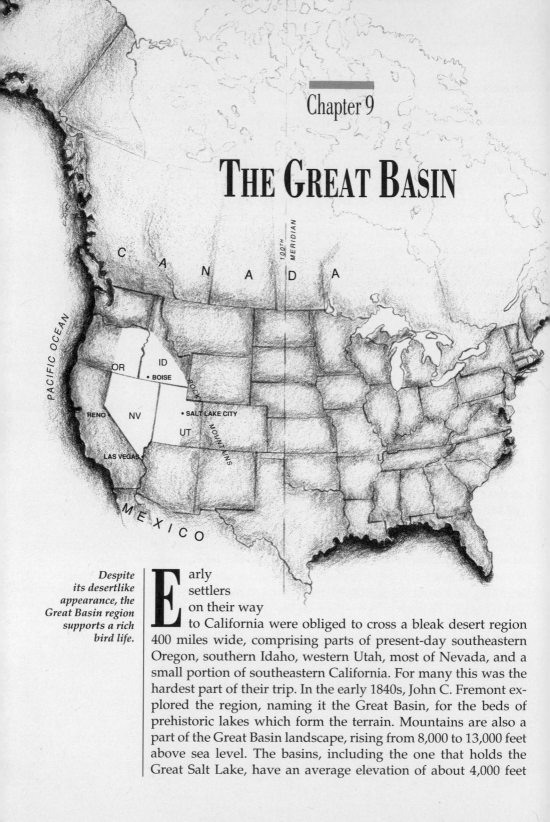

Chapter 9

THE GREAT BASIN

Despite its desertlike appearance, the Great Basin region supports a rich bird life.

Early settlers on their way to California were obliged to cross a bleak desert region 400 miles wide, comprising parts of present-day southeastern Oregon, southern Idaho, western Utah, most of Nevada, and a small portion of southeastern California. For many this was the hardest part of their trip. In the early 1840s, John C. Fremont explored the region, naming it the Great Basin, for the beds of prehistoric lakes which form the terrain. Mountains are also a part of the Great Basin landscape, rising from 8,000 to 13,000 feet above sea level. The basins, including the one that holds the Great Salt Lake, have an average elevation of about 4,000 feet above sea level.

The Great Basin region is about half desert, with the remainder a mixture of foothills and mountains. The deserts are cold in winter and burning hot in summer. The frigid winters have earned them the name "cold desert," in contrast with hot deserts such as the Mojave to the south. One reason this region is so arid is that it lies in the shadow of high mountain ranges to the west. As storm systems blow inland from the Pacific, the western mountains coax nearly all the precipitation out of the fronts, meaning the Great Basin, except for its higher peaks, is cut off from normal rainfall. The desert regions receive only five to ten inches of precipitation a year.

Arid conditions and drastic seasonal temperature changes have not prevented the Great Basin from having a rich avifauna. Its bird life is described by Fred A. Ryser, Jr., in his book *Birds of the Great Basin*. Among the more common birds are the Gambel's quail, sage grouse, mourning dove, black-billed magpie, common raven, sage thrasher, house finch, lark sparrow, black-throated sparrow, and Brewer's blackbird. That some of the birds have a common name containing the word "sage" is appropriate. The sagebrushes (*Artemisia*) are the dominant plants of the deserts and lower mountain slopes, providing vital cover and food for wildlife. The sage grouse, for example, subsists almost entirely upon the foliage of the native sagebrushes.

Birdbaths are very attractive to birds in the arid Great Basin. Here a black-headed grosbeak takes a dip.

Birds living in the desert have adapted in various ways to the near absence of water. As Fred Ryser points out, some birds fly long distances to procure water. This is true of the mourning dove, which, if it has to, makes a long early morning flight to water and another late in the day. The black-throated sparrow obtains nearly all the water it needs from its food. Its normal diet consists of insects and the foliage of plants.

Enough rainfall reaches higher mountain slopes within the Great Basin to maintain forest growth much like that in the Rockies or other western mountain ranges. Higher life zones contain such species as the Clark's nutcracker, Cassin's finch, evening grosbeak, and rosy finch.

Human beings, with their irrigation and plantings, have modified the harsh conditions wherever they have settled. The bird life in cities like Reno, Salt Lake City, and Boise is much the same as in other western cities at the same altitude and latitude. All have starlings, house sparrows, and house finches. But game birds are a little more conspicuous in Great Basin towns and cities. The California quail, introduced from its native state, thrives in densely populated areas. Writing of this quail in the Reno area, Fred Ryser states: "Everywhere, small to large coveys are seen, often afoot, running across city streets or filtering across lawns. The coveys repeatedly visit feeding stations where birdseed is available."

In more northern parts of the Great Basin, the ring-necked pheasant is common in agricultural districts. On the other hand, the chukar, another introduced game bird, prefers bleak desert country far from human habitations. State game departments assist this bird by building cisterns or "guzzlers" in desert country that catch the rainfall and supply water to game birds and other desert species.

Southwestern Utah

With a little irrigation the desert can offer a rich habitat for birds. This is demonstrated by Jewel A. Gifford, who, living at an altitude of 3,900 feet in southwestern Utah, has attracted nearly 40 species to her feeders and to plantings in her yard. Water in birdbaths, as well as sunflower seed, chicken scratch feed, suet, and sugar water at feeders provide a combination that birds cannot resist.

Springdale, Utah, where she lives, is close enough to the hot deserts of the Southwest to be within the range limits of the Gambel's quail, blue grosbeak, rufous-crowned sparrow, and black-chinned sparrow, all of which appear at her feeders. The black-chinned sparrow is a shy bird of dense chaparral and sagebrush that rarely visits feeding stations. An even more unexpected visitor is the Scott's oriole. A single specimen has appeared at her sugar water feeders.

Hummingbirds are not as plentiful or represented by as many species as in regions closer to Mexico. Ms. Gifford's sugar water feeders, however, are visited by resident black-chinned and broad-tailed hummingbirds and by migrant rufous hummingbirds. They also attract northern orioles and western tanagers.

Among her more common feeder birds are mourning doves, scrub jays, black-capped and mountain chickadees, black-headed grosbeaks, lazuli buntings, green-tailed and rufous-sided towhees, white-crowned and song sparrows, red-winged blackbirds, Cassin's finches, and house finches.

Western Great Basin

On the opposite side of the Great Basin at Lake Tahoe on the Nevada-California border, Greg Scyphers has very different

birds at his feeders from those at Jewel Gifford's. She complains that she has no woodpeckers or nuthatches. But at 6,400 feet on the Nevada side of the lake, Mr. Scyphers has northern flickers, white-headed woodpeckers, and white-breasted, red-breasted, and pygmy nuthatches coming to his suet feeders.

He is one of the few people to be successful in attracting the wary white-headed woodpecker to a feeding station. Found from northern Idaho and Washington southward to western Nevada and southern California, the white-headed woodpecker is a strikingly handsome bird of higher elevations, closely associated with ponderosa pine and other conifers. In both altitude and habitat, Mr. Scyphers is perfectly located for attracting these woodpeckers. Among the conifers that grow in the vicinity of his home are ponderosa, Jeffrey, and lodgepole pines and the Douglas fir.

Eastern Great Basin

On the eastern side of the Great Basin, Salt Lake City, at an altitude of 4,600 feet, scarcely fits a description of the Great Basin. Its green lawns and shade trees contrast sharply with the desert country that stretches westward, from the Great Salt Lake to the Sierra Nevada in California. The bird life of this attractive city reminds one of Denver. Birds typical of both the high plains and of the mountains are present, the latter being more in evidence in winter. Feeders operated by Mrs. George Proctor in one part of the city and William Pratt in another are visited by mourning doves, Steller's jays, black-capped chickadees, northern orioles, evening grosbeaks, dark-eyed (Oregon) juncos, and house sparrows. Lazuli buntings appear at Mr. Pratt's feeders in spring, and his sugar water feeders are patronized by broad-tailed hummingbirds. Trumpet creeper in his yard offers a source of nectar for hummingbirds, and bush honeysuckle and Nanking cherry provide fruit for robins.

At the eastern edge of the Great Basin, Mr. and Mrs. Rex B. Snow of Bountiful Bench, to the north of Salt Lake City, provide a different list of birds likely to visit feeders. California quail and ring-necked pheasants compete here with each other for seeds and grain at feeding stations, with as many as 300 quail possible during the course of a day. Besides common visitors, such as dark-eyed (Oregon) juncos and white-crowned sparrows, the Snows have had downy woodpeckers, brown creepers, and Townsend's solitaires at their feeders.

North-Central Great Basin

In southwestern Idaho, where the Snake River has cut a broad valley in the high country through which it flows, the altitude is lower than in most other parts of the Great Basin. With the help of irrigation, this part of Idaho has been turned into a rich agricultural area containing many towns and a few small cities. At Caldwell, near the state capital of Boise, Mrs. Elizabeth Montgomery has had success at bird feeding.

Using sunflower, thistle, and—for Steller's jays—peanuts, she has about the same birds coming to her Caldwell feeders as those at feeders in Salt Lake City, 350 miles to the south. Despite its lower altitude (2,400 feet), Caldwell has colder winter temperatures than Salt Lake City, with the mercury reaching as low as 26° below zero on some days. To help birds through frigid spells, Mrs. Montgomery offers extra food, grit, and water in a heated birdbath. Among her winter patrons are mourning doves, occasional blue jays, Steller's jays, black-capped chickadees, house finches, pine siskins, evening grosbeaks, and house sparrows. Lazuli buntings arrive in spring and visit the feeders. The black-chinned hummingbird is common in summer at her sugar water feeders.

At a mountain cabin (elevation 5,200 feet) where she also feeds birds, Mrs. Montgomery reports the rufous and Calliope hummingbirds to be common visitors to her sugar water feeders. Seeds and grain bring mountain chickadees, Cassin's finches, pine siskins, evening grosbeaks, chipping sparrows, and dark-eyed (Oregon) juncos. Some of the birds that visit her cabin and home in Caldwell somehow overlook her food offerings. This is true of the northern flicker, starling, yellow warbler, western tanager, and rufous-sided (spotted) towhee. Likewise, cedar and

Bohemian waxwings visit her crabapple trees for fruit on their way south in the fall, but ignore any offerings at her feeders.

Special Birds

There is not a single bird species that is endemic to the Great Basin. All of the species found within its confines also occur in other parts of the West, or, in the case of some, widely throughout much of North America. But a few species are more apt to appear at bird feeders in this region than in other parts of their range. This is especially true of the lazuli bunting, one of the West's more colorful birds and one that is sometimes indifferent to feeder fare. The same is true of the western tanager and lesser goldfinch, which even in the Great Basin do not respond well to food, though both come readily to water. Jewel Gifford in Springdale, Utah, found that lesser goldfinches came to sunflower seeds on heads of plants growing in her yard and to evening primrose and elm seeds. She has had a very good response to the fruits of mulberry trees in her yard. Among the birds that relish them are band-tailed pigeons, grosbeaks and orioles of several kinds, and phainopeplas. The latter, at its northern range limits in southern Utah, is not a feeder bird.

Gambel's quail and California quail are highly receptive to food offerings wherever they are found. But in the Great Basin region they seem even more forward about coming to feeders in towns and cities. Large coveys make the rounds of residential areas looking for food. Ranges of the two rarely overlap, the Gambel's being found in the southern portions of the Great Ba-

Gambel's quail usually visit a feeder in a covey of several birds.

sin and the California in the northern.

Previously mentioned white-headed woodpeckers at Greg Scyphers' feeders at Lake Tahoe and black-chinned sparrows at Jewel Gifford's feeders in Springdale supply still other records of success with hard-to-attract birds. Although there is ample satisfaction in feeding birds that everyone has at their feeders, a certain thrill comes from attracting birds that are unexpected.

Food and Cover Plants for Birds

In the Great Basin region, where there is little water to spare, it is important to know about plants—both native and introduced—that are capable of enduring hot summers, cold winters, and lack of moisture. One of the best plants is Russian olive, a small tree that has the ability to withstand desertlike conditions. The Siberian pea tree (*Caragana arborescens*) is another good candidate. It can be used as both a windbreak and as cover for wildlife, though it does not provide food for birds.

A plant which provides food, cover, and is a good ornamental for our yards is the russet buffalo-berry (*Shepherdia canadensis*). This plant has silvery gray-green foliage and in early summer, bears large clusters of red berries.

Other plant families resistant to the Great Basin's harsh conditions are wild lilacs (*Ceanothus*), junipers, smaller pines, manzanitas, cotoneasters, and yuccas.

Special Problems

In arid regions, more than in wetter ones, there is a serious penalty to be paid for the destruction of native vegetation. This applies equally well throughout much of the West where farming and ranching have drastically altered the environment. Fire, over-grazing, and conversion of original habitat to other purposes by humans are the chief threats to native plant growth. The native sagebrushes of the Great Basin, vitally important in supplying food and cover for birds and wildlife, and in preventing erosion, should be preserved whenever possible. The same holds true for the pinyon pine and juniper on higher slopes. Wherever this cover is removed, the desert birds, along with many other unique forms of wildlife, disappear. If you plan to plant your property to attract native birds and wildlife, remember that the best place to start is with native plants, shrubs, and trees. □

Suspended sunflower heads provide an easy meal for several lesser goldfinches.

127

**The
Great Basin**

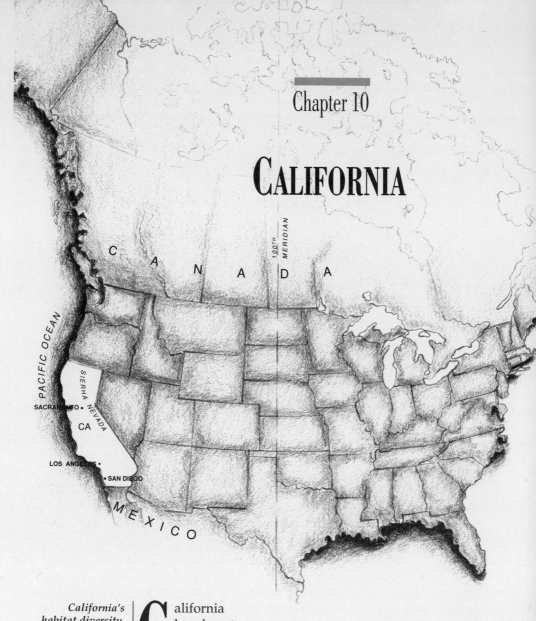

Chapter 10

CALIFORNIA

*California's
habitat diversity,
temperate climate,
and location on a
migration flyway
make bird feeding
an exciting
activity.*

C alifornia
has deserts
and high mountains,
and a long coastline facing the Pacific Ocean. With its
many habitats, including a large number of human-made ones,
the state easily offers as much diversity as anywhere in the West.
In the eastern part, the Sierra Nevada meets the Cascade Mountains, which extend southward from Oregon. The Sierras stretch
southward to the Mojave Desert. Both ranges have peaks over
14,000 feet in altitude. Parallel mountain ranges having somewhat lower elevations lie near the coast. The Coastal Ranges, as

they are called, reach from Oregon south to Los Angeles. Between the eastern and western mountains lies the rich Central Valley with its ranch and agricultural lands. Other mountains appear in the southernmost part of the state and continue southward into the long, arid Baja Peninsula, a part of Mexico. In short, California is one of the most exciting parts of the country for bird watching and bird feeding.

Here, as elsewhere in the West, both the plant and animal life change with every thousand feet or so in elevation. But in winter many of the mountain birds appear at lower elevations and come to our bird feeders. Together with permanent residents and birds that arrive from the north, they assure variety at feeders—something that most people welcome. Regardless of the seasons, California bird feeders are likely to be patronized by at least one kind of dove, one or two kinds of jays, the inevitable house sparrows and house finches, and one or two pairs of California towhees.

For those who feed hummingbirds, the Anna's hummingbird is present nearly everywhere all year and five or six other hummingbirds can be counted upon either as migrants or breeding birds. These expected species, along with strays from Mexico, make hummingbird feeding almost as exciting in California as it is in the mountains of New Mexico and Arizona. As everywhere in the West, sugar water is also a major attraction for house finches, orioles, and many other birds.

I am confining my treatment of California to the central valleys and coastal regions. This is where most of the people live and consequently where most of the bird feeding is conducted. For those who live in the mountains to the east, bird feeding is very much the same as it is in the Rockies (see Chapter 8). For the more arid parts of southern California, reference should be made to bird feeding in the similar habitats of Arizona and New Mexico (see Chapter 7).

One of California's most familiar feeder birds is the California (brown) towhee.

Avian Abundance

Visiting Los Angeles and its outlying suburbs in December one year, I was impressed by how abundant the bird life was. Robins and cedar waxwings were thronging through the trees and descending in large flocks to feed upon berry-bearing shrubs. The shrubs in turn were being defended by mockingbirds that were just as aggressive here as anywhere else in North America. Raucous calls of scrub jays echoed above the traffic and told me that this jay was as common in the city as it was on forested mountain slopes. The titmouse I heard calling was the plain titmouse, and a small woodpecker that looked like a downy was the Nuttall's woodpecker. I was almost certain that the hummingbird I saw in so many yards was the Anna's.

In downtown parks, spotted doves of Old World origin vied for food with domestic pigeons. Equally at home in parks or residential areas were brown towhees (now called the California towhee in this part of its range), house sparrows, and Brewer's blackbirds. Only one other bird seemed more numerous and widespread. This was the house finch, a California native which had not yet begun its epic spread throughout much of the rest of North America.

A Way of Life

Bird feeding is a way of life for many Californians. To have birds in the yard and visiting feeders and birdbaths is as enjoyable as having gardens, flower beds, and swimming pools. This does not mean that one has to be affluent to feed birds. On a smaller scale, people who live in apartments or small homes enjoy this form of entertainment.

Birds have always responded well to overtures made in their behalf in California. The first experiments in feeding hummingbirds were conducted in the state, and the first waterfowl feeding program was started here (see Chapter 1). Like watching the swallows come back to Capistrano, feeding is a way to welcome birds as they return from the tropics in the spring or arrive from the mountains or the north in the fall.

Yet in California there is little sense of urgency about feeding birds during certain seasons. This is especially true near the coast with its temperate year-round climate. As a result most people are in the habit of feeding birds all year. Through letters and questionnaires I have discovered just how true this is. Close to 100 percent of those queried feed birds the entire year and surprisingly, everyone who feeds birds also feeds hummingbirds all year. This contrasts sharply with many other parts of the country where bird feeding is initiated in the fall and ends about the time the last migrants have departed northward in the spring.

The Hummingbirds

Bird feeding and hummingbird feeding are practically synonymous in California. Of seven hummingbird species that nest in the state, the Anna's is by far the most common. It obliges us by being present the entire year. According to John Walters of

the San Diego Audubon Society, between 95 and 99 percent of the hummingbirds seen in his part of southern California are Anna's. Although largely a desert species, the Costa's hummingbird also nests in urban districts in southern California and is present in winter in small numbers. A third species present in winter, the Allen's hummingbird, is a spring and fall migrant and nests from Ventura in southern California northward to southwestern Oregon. At about its northern range limits, the Allen's is replaced by its close relative the rufous hummingbird, which nests from northern California all the way to southwestern Alaska. The rufous, as well as the Calliope and black-chinned, are present over much of California as spring and fall migrants. The black-chinned hummingbird nests from southern California northward and the Calliope from central California northward.

Up until about 30 years ago, the Anna's hummingbird was considered to be one of California's birds that rarely wandered outside the state. But, beginning in the mid-1960s, the Anna's began a remarkable range expansion that took it to Alaska, other western states, and in fall and winter as far east as the Gulf Coast in Texas and Louisiana.

What initiated this immigration? A permanent resident, the Anna's had formerly only made short seasonal movements to the mountains. Virginia C. Holmgren, in her book *The Way of the Hummingbird*, advances the theory that brush fires, floods, and mud slides in California during the mid-1960s destroyed so much of the Anna's habitat that hungry and homeless birds had no choice but to leave. A second view is that this was a case of

Perhaps the most abundant feeder bird in California is the house finch.

range expansion brought on by population pressure. A third view is that wild populations, if they are healthy, will expand whenever they have the opportunity—and human-made alterations of habitat provided the opportunity for the Anna's hummingbird. Whatever the reason, those that left apparently did not return. Relying upon hummingbird feeders and natural foods, they survived as best they could in their new homes. First recorded in the state of Washington in 1964, it wasn't long before the Anna's was nesting in warmer coastal districts both there and in British Columbia. But some of those who were playing host to Anna's were making the mistake of taking their hummingbird feeders down when they thought it was time for the birds to depart southward. They didn't realize that this was a hummingbird that, unlike the others, did not migrate south in the fall. People are now being urged to keep on offering food as long as any hummingbirds are in evidence.

The Anna's is well-adapted to cold conditions. Norm and Maggie Mellor of Corona, California, write that they have observed Anna's where they visit in the mountains, surviving daytime temperatures as low as 22° F. and at night as low as 9° F. Like other hummingbirds, the Anna's conserves its energy during periods of cold or stress by lowering its body temperature and going into a state of torpor.

Hummingbird Plants

For those who wish to help hummingbirds by providing natural sources of nectar for them, there is a wide range of plants that can be grown in California. These include introduced trees, such as eucalyptus, silk oak (*Grevillea robusta*), and the bottlebrushes (*Callistemon*) from Australia. Another introduced plant, tree tobacco (*Nicotiana glauca*) from South America, is widely naturalized in the southern part of the state and an almost year-round source of food for hummers. According to Virgil J. Ketner of Ventura, both the salvias and Cape honeysuckle (*Tecomaria capensis*) from South Africa, furnish food the entire year.

The best of the sages for southern California is Mexican sage (*Salvia leucantha*). Other sages, including pineapple sage (*S. elegans*), are excellent hummingbird plants. One native California plant is so well-liked by hummingbirds that it is called hummingbird flower. Also called California fuchsia (*Zauschneria californica*), it is a handsome plant that can be grown easily in the garden. This plant is not to be confused with the true fuchsias, which are also good hummingbird plants. Where the winter is mild, true fuchsias can be grown outdoors, and their bright blossoms are often seen emanating from plants in hanging baskets.

Still other good choices are rosemary, coralbells, penstemon, speedwell, bee balm, hibiscus, aloes, the honeysuckles (*Lonicera*), and, for those who live near citrus groves or have the trees in their yard, the blossoms of the orange tree. During the period when the trees are in bloom, hummingbirds usually desert sugar water feeders for this plentiful source of nectar.

Other Feeder Birds

Many Californians who feed birds are fortunate enough to play host to the state bird, the California quail. These striking birds are often seen trooping in one by one to settle down to a session of feeding, leaving one of their kind perched nearby as a lookout. A true native, this quail has a range stretching from southern Oregon southward through the Baja Peninsula. It has also been introduced to other parts of the West.

One dove present in many yards in southern California is the spotted dove, an exotic introduced from the Old World.

The thrasher with the long, sickle-shaped bill that usually is seen feeding below a feeder is the California thrasher. A native of the two Californias (the state and Baja), it replaces the curve-billed thrasher of Arizona and New Mexico.

At most feeding stations it won't take long to find the California towhee, the drab brown bird that frequents our landscaped habitats. It is a common visitor to bird feeders and the

Bird feeding is a relaxing backyard activity for many people.

*Black-chinned
hummers visit
California feeders
in spring, summer,
and fall.*

California counterpart of the canyon towhee of the Southwest.

With the possible exception of the black-headed grosbeak, there aren't any other birds resembling the cardinals and pyrrhuloxias that frequent feeders in Arizona, but Californians do feed a number of distinctive sparrows. The small sparrow with the black whisker mark is the rufous-crowned that ranges as far east as western Arkansas. California has a separate population made up of several races. One of them is known as the California rufous-crowned sparrow. The fox and song sparrows of the West Coast are divided into even more races, each with slightly different coloration. A visiting Easterner would scarcely recognize them as belonging to the same species common in the East. The fox sparrows are dusky brown instead of reddish and the song sparrows much paler in the desert races and much darker in the more northern types.

The crowned sparrows, frequent feeder visitors, are largish, plump birds with distinctive head and facial markings. The white-crowned sparrow, the most common member of the group, nests in more northern parts of the state and along with others from the north makes up the large sparrow flocks that are seen in winter. The white-crowneds are joined by golden-crowned sparrows that have come down from the north. Two other crowned sparrows, the white-throated and Harris', are regular strays this far west, seen with increasing frequency in recent winters.

Not all of California's distinctive birds are as easy to see as those already mentioned. The wrentit, an elusive bird of dense chaparral thickets, is more easily heard than seen, but it does sometimes visit feeding stations. Chiefly coastal in its range, it is found from northwestern Oregon southward to northern Baja.

Two species that might be expected to visit feeding stations are conspicuously absent as visitors. One, the Lawrence's goldfinch, is almost exclusively a California bird but hard to find even in the southern part of the state where it is most plentiful. John Walters says it is a "red-letter day" to see one. "They seem to be an unusually restless species. Here today, gone tomorrow." The second standoffish species is the tricolored blackbird, which nests in large colonies and has limited ranges in southern Oregon and California. Of this species, Walters says "It is somewhat similar to the Lawrence's goldfinch in being a very restless species with a shifting distribution. You rarely see just one; it's usually a whole flock." The tricolored is apparently the only blackbird that does not take advantage of the food offerings provided by humans.

One other native Californian, the yellow-billed magpie of the central valleys and foothills, is easy to find within its range, though, like the black-billed magpie, it is more of a wayside scavenger than a feeder bird. They can sometimes be lured to a suet feeder.

Foods for Feeder Birds

It takes the right food or foods to attract the species we want at our bird feeders. Marge West of Half Moon Bay, south of San Francisco, began offering niger at a special feeder in hopes of attracting the American goldfinches that nested in her yard. Instead pine siskins immediately claimed the niger, and the goldfinches went to hanging feeders with black oil sunflower seeds. When I visited the West residence in October, 1988, a steady stream of siskins was coming all day for the niger. Only the occasional presence of a hawk over a nearby pasture kept them away.

Mrs. West told me that several hundred pine siskins visited her feeders year-round. This population was augmented by others that arrived from the north in the fall and suddenly departed in the spring. Probably as many house finches were also year-round visitors. Their tastes ran to the black oil sunflower seeds and halved cantaloupe made available at a special feeder. Red-winged blackbirds and brown-headed cowbirds confined their feeding primarily to sprays of millet fastened to raised feeders and to food on the ground. A variety of foods, including a cornmeal/peanut butter mix, at a number of feeders served to reduce competition. Even the feisty pine siskins left other birds alone as long as they did not come to the niger feeders.

Unusual visitors to the West's feeders included a yellow-headed blackbird, a Nanday conure, and a red weaver. The latter two birds were undoubtedly escaped cage birds, probably attracted by the parrots and cockatiels kept by Mrs. West.

When not tending to the needs of her birds—wild ones and caged—Mrs. West spends many hours working as a volunteer at a bird rehabilitation center. For the Wests, feeding and tending to birds is a way of life, just as it is for so many Californians.

Survey results showed that sunflower seed, including shelled meats, black oil, and striped, is the food most commonly used by Californians at their feeding stations. Sugar water, both for hummingbirds and the many other birds that respond to a sweetish solution, was a close second. Mixed wild birdseeds (the type often available at the supermarket) ranked third in favor.

Suet and suet mixes were in fourth place, closely followed by niger and cracked corn. Peanuts in the shell were popular with those who fed jays. A few respondents complained that sorghum (including milo), cracked corn, wheat, and millet were not always eaten.

Plants for Food and Shelter

In a way, California is like a botanical garden with its many plants from all over the world. They include pyracantha, bottlebrush, cotoneasters, tree tobacco, rosemary, and English ivy—all good bird food plants. At the same time, there are many handsome native plants that serve the same purpose and can be grown more widely. Toyon or Christmas berry is an evergreen shrub or small tree that produces bright red berries which are readily eaten by birds. Native junipers provide both food and shelter for birds—the blue waxy fruits are a source of food for birds in winter. The native mahonias are handsome evergreens with fruit well-liked by birds.

Native elderberries deserve more consideration for their ornamental qualities, their juicy fruits for making preserves, and their popularity with birds. Blue elderberry (*Sambucus glauca*) is heavily laden with blue fruit in the fall. There are others to choose from that have either red or purple-black fruit. A beautiful evergreen tree, madrone (*Arbutus menziesii*) of California's mountains also has a place in the yard. Its red or orange berries are eaten by birds in fall and winter.

I recommend many of these same plants in Chapter 11 on the Pacific Northwest. Along with native pines and oaks they provide food and shelter for birds and are handsome ornamentals. In California there is no shortage of good plants to use—both native and introduced—to feed the birds.

Special Problems

Questionnaire responses indicate that the house cat is considered to be more troublesome in California at bird feeders than any other mammal. There were few complaints about possums, raccoons, chipmunks, and ground squirrels. The gray squirrel was considered to be a nuisance, but twice as many people complained about house cats.

Why this sentiment about a pet that many bird lovers own and which can often be trusted in yards where birds are fed? Probably the answer is that some cats are bird killers and others are not. The blame usually seems to lie with the neighbor's cats or feral cats that obtain food in any way they can. Smaller, more trusting birds seem to suffer the most.

The pine siskin is especially susceptible to losses from cats. Marge West, who feeds such large numbers of siskins throughout the year, places both her thistle feeders and birdbaths as high as she can. Out of reach of cats the siskins can eat and bathe in relative safety.

Even hummingbirds, as seen in reports from several localities, are sometimes preyed upon by cats. A cat is capable of leaping several feet into the air, and, if quick enough, can catch a hummingbird as it hovers near a feeder. Mary Roth of San Diego reported that a neighbor had two cats that frequently caught hummingbirds.

During the nesting season, ground-nesting birds, such as quail and the rufous-sided towhee, are particularly vulnerable to being preyed upon by cats and other predators. Donald R. Clark of Bolinas has a covey of around 30 California quail coming to his feeders all year. However, he states that there would be many more of the birds if it were not for predation by cats.

As long as there are cats present, birds at our feeders will be vulnerable. But commonsense solutions, such as placing feeders in the open so birds can see approaching danger and raising feeders and baths up out of reach of cats, will make our yards safer for our avian guests. □

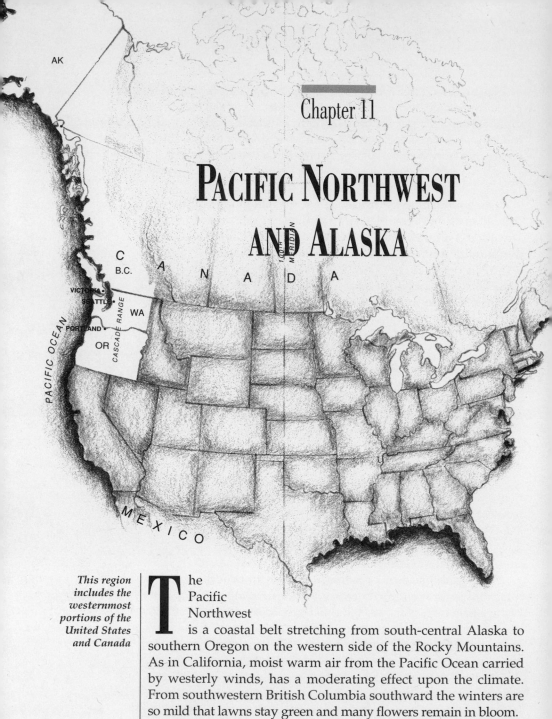

Chapter 11

PACIFIC NORTHWEST AND ALASKA

AK

C
B.C.

C A N A D A

VICTORIA
SEATTLE
PORTLAND

WA

CASCADE RANGE

OR

PACIFIC OCEAN

100TH MERIDIAN

M E X I C O

This region includes the westernmost portions of the United States and Canada

The Pacific Northwest is a coastal belt stretching from south-central Alaska to southern Oregon on the western side of the Rocky Mountains. As in California, moist warm air from the Pacific Ocean carried by westerly winds, has a moderating effect upon the climate. From southwestern British Columbia southward the winters are so mild that lawns stay green and many flowers remain in bloom.

In Oregon the topography is much the same as it is in California. The Coast Ranges hug the coast and the Cascade Mountains, lying parallel to them to the east, are regarded as the eastern boundary of the Pacific Northwest. In northern Oregon, the

Willamette Valley lies between the two mountain ranges. The Coast Ranges follow the coast only as far north as the mouth of the Columbia River, but the Cascades continue into northern Washington where they merge with the Rockies. The bird life of the Cascades is much the same as that of the Rockies.

Cool summers and mild winters make it possible for many bird species to become year-round residents. As a result there are not the pronounced seasonal changes at bird feeders that are seen where the summers are hot, the winters cold.

The conditions that enable many of the birds to remain through the year also provide pleasant living conditions for humans. Large cities, such as Portland, Oregon, Seattle, Washington, and Vancouver, British Columbia, and smaller ones, like Olympia, Washington, and Eugene, Oregon, are garden spots where birds are plentiful and bird feeding is a popular hobby.

Bird Life

Besides birds that are permanent residents, the Pacific Northwest plays host to migrants that arrive in spring to nest, and depart southward in the fall. Another group is made up of birds that nest in the mountains and descend to lower elevations when the winter weather is harsh. A number of birds from more eastern parts of the country travel to the mild coastal belt to pass the winter. Often regarded as strays, these birds include the blue jay, brown thrasher, and white-throated and Harris' sparrows.

Among the species unique to this region are the northwestern crow, the varied thrush, and the chestnut-backed chickadee. Not a typical feeder bird, the northwestern crow is the tamest of any of the crows. It will come readily to bread and other scraps tossed its way. Its entire range lies in a narrow coastal belt from southern Alaska to the Puget Sound, near Seattle, Washington.

An already rich avifauna has been added to by introductions made by humans. Two of them are the well-known house sparrow and European starling brought to our shores during the last century and which found their way into the West. The house sparrow was first seen in Seattle in 1897 and the starling reached the West Coast during the 1950s. Both are all too familiar at feeders. The crested myna, a member of the starling family, was brought to Vancouver, British Columbia, in 1897 and never moved far beyond its release point. The European skylark, which became established in the southern part of Vancouver Island, also failed to spread very far. Two introduced game birds—the ring-necked pheasant and California quail—are

Rufous hummingbirds nest throughout the Pacific Northwest, and as far north as Alaska.

firmly established in the region and will occasionally visit feeding stations.

Native west coast species which have expanded their ranges into the Pacific Northwest include the Anna's hummingbird, scrub jay, northern mockingbird, and house finch. One long-time resident, the northern (Bullock's) oriole, is experiencing a population boom.

Altogether an exciting place to feed birds, the Pacific Northwest has its expected species and others whose presence depends upon natural food supplies and the severity of the weather. A poor fruit and conifer seed harvest in the mountains will result in many more birds than usual at feeding stations at lower elevations. Cold and snow will have the same result. One year, when visiting western Oregon in late fall, I encountered large flocks of varied thrushes wherever I went. This many birds at lower elevations suggested that winter had come early in the mountains and that there may have been food shortages as well.

Bird Feeding in Seattle

Located on Puget Sound in northwestern Washington, Seattle is a city of parks, lakes, islands, and a moderate year-round climate. Late fall, winter, and spring constitute the wet season; rarely does it snow, and freezing temperatures are unusual. Nevertheless, many birds seem to rely heavily upon the extra food they obtain at bird feeding stations.

On Mercer Island, an eastern suburb of Seattle, bird feeding is conducted against a background of tall conifers, sparkling lake waters, and snow-capped mountains. Among those who have been feeding birds for years amid this setting are Thero North, George Johnson, and Lee Norwood. They and others see to it that the island's small permanent population of Anna's hummingbirds holds its own. With the help of sugar water, small flying insects, and late flowers, such as fuchsias, *sarcococca* (a small evergreen shrub with tiny white flowers), winter-blooming camellias, and winter jasmine, the birds survive even during occasional periods of cold weather. The rufous hummingbird is present from mid-March through early summer. Tiny bushtits visit yards and gardens but rarely patronize bird feeders. Townsend's warblers are more expected at bird feeders during the winter than the commoner yellow-rumped warbler. Small birds such as these sometimes appear at feeders at the same time with California quail and band-tailed pigeons.

At Mrs. North's feeders, chestnut-backed chickadees visit

window feeders, whereas the larger, more aggressive black-capped chickadees go to hanging tubular feeders and beautifully constructed gazebo-type feeders well away from the house. Keen competitors, the two chickadees tend to go their separate ways, though both are fearless so far as their human benefactors are concerned. Mrs. North, and others who feed birds on the island, can count upon still other year-round visitors to their yards and feeders. Very much in evidence are the Steller's jays, red-breasted nuthatches, Bewick's wrens, American robins, rufous-sided (spotted) towhees, house finches, American goldfinches, pine siskins, dark-eyed (Oregon) juncos, and fox, white-crowned, and song sparrows.

Jeanette Urbain, who feeds birds in a western part of Seattle, has many of the same birds that throng feeders on Mercer Island. She has better luck than most people with bushtits. Two or three dozen of the tiny birds visit the peanut butter suet cakes at her feeders three or four times daily. They trickle in one behind the other until they completely cover the feeders where they are eating. Anna's hummingbirds take turns visiting her sugar water feeders and the flowers in her yard. From early spring into early summer, rufous hummingbirds are also present. She believes that it is difficult to attract hummers with feeders alone. There must also be blooming flowers of the species that appeal to hummingbirds.

British Columbia

Only 100 miles north of Seattle is the city of Vancouver, British Columbia. It overlooks an arm of the Pacific and has the same mild climate as Seattle. According to Brian Self, who feeds birds in Vancouver, snow is infrequent and some winters there

The chestnut-backed chickadee is a resident of the coniferous forests of the Pacific Northwest.

is none at all. He states that by mid-February winter is over and snowdrops and crocuses are in bloom. It is no wonder that many birds fail to migrate or have become permanent residents. In winter one finds Anna's hummingbirds, American robins, Bewick's and winter wrens, kinglets, red-winged blackbirds, and rufous-sided (spotted) towhees in the Vancouver area. All are birds that in other parts of the West, winter far to the south.

The same bird species that visit feeders in Seattle are also present at feeders in Vancouver. Among the birds coming to black oil sunflower seed at feeders maintained by Brian Self are black-capped and chestnut-backed chickadees, pine siskins, evening grosbeaks, purple finches, and a relative newcomer, the house finch. Responding to a question of mine about the crested myna, he stated that the population is at an all-time low. He cited competition by the European starling as the reason. I recall that on a visit to Vancouver in 1957, I found the birds at several places in the city where they responded well to bread but ignored grain.

Jessie Law, who lives in a suburb of Vancouver, has had exceptionally good luck attracting birds with suet. Among the birds coming to her feeders for suet have been downy and pileated woodpeckers, the two chickadees, bushtits, and, in the fall, winter wrens. She also supplies mixed birdseed and sunflower seed. Birds take turns for the food. First to come are the chickadees, then juncos, followed by starlings, Steller's jays, flickers, and, most shy of all, varied thrushes. If crows arrive, all the birds leave the feeding station area.

The city of Victoria on Vancouver Island, 45 miles to the west of Vancouver, is equally well situated for year-round bird feeding. Anna's hummingbirds are present all year and feeders are patronized by the same birds that are found on the mainland. Dr. R. Wayne Campbell of the Royal British Columbia Museum at Victoria has recorded no fewer than 41 species at his feeders over the 28-year period that he has been feeding birds. With Harold Hosford, he co-authored a booklet called *Attracting and Feeding Birds in British Columbia* (Published by the British Columbia Provincial Museum, Victoria, B.C. 1979). The publication contains good information on plantings, food, feeders, use of water, and birdhouses.

The authors recommend planting red-flowering currant (*Ribes sanguineum*) for its early blossoms, which invite hummingbirds, and for the bluish berries which appear later and are eaten by a wide variety of birds. The same advantages can be obtained from orange honeysuckle (*Lonicera ciliosa*), a trailing vine with orange flowers. The flowers attract hummingbirds in the spring, and the berries, which are orange-red, attract birds in the fall. Even pyracantha can be grown in warmer portions of the province. Campbell and Hosford suggest the presence of winter-flowering jasmine, with its early blossoms, as one reason why Anna's hummingbirds are able to spend the winter in the southwestern coastal regions of the Pacific Northwest.

Besides feeding birds in their yards, many people, according to Dr. Campbell, also feed waterfowl, gulls, pheasants, northwestern crows, and even bald eagles. The latter are given herring thrown from wharves and fishing piers.

Bird Feeding in Alaska

North of Vancouver the coastal region becomes mountainous and far less inviting to birds during the colder months. This is equally true in the southern panhandle of Alaska 500 miles to the north. However, this northern region offers some surprises.

Ralph B. Williams, who once fed and banded birds in Alaska's capital of Juneau, wrote me that "physiological changes in the birds themselves make it possible for them to stand subzero temperatures as long as they can get food as fuel." Listing sources of food available to birds in the vicinity of Juneau, he reports that worms, insects, and other small forms of animal life are present in snow-free areas on tidal flats and stream banks along the coast. He adds that seeds of spruce and alder, as well as tree buds, furnish food for a number of birds.

During some winters, according to Williams, the Juneau area is invaded by immense flocks of rosy finches belonging to the gray-crowned race. They attend feeding stations where canary seeds and bread crumbs are offered, and are so tame that a person can walk into a flock feeding on the ground without causing the birds to fly. The flocks remind him of a swarm of giant bees. At night the rosy finches take shelter in the nests of cliff swallows—a habit that has been reported elsewhere.

Even as far north as Fairbanks bird feeding is rewarding. Fairbanks is in central Alaska, approximately 100 miles south of

Varied thrushes.

AK •FAIRBANKS

•ANCHORAGE

•JUNEAU

Harsh winters in Alaska make bird feeding especially rewarding for both birds and people.

the Arctic Circle. John Leipzig, who feeds birds from September until May in a forested area near Fairbanks, has downy and hairy woodpeckers, gray jays, black-capped and boreal chickadees, common and hoary redpolls, and pine grosbeaks at his feeders. Foods offered include black oil sunflower seed, niger, suet, cornbread, and other scraps. Gray jays come mainly for the scraps. Mr. Leipzig states that the rufous hummingbird rarely appears this far north. He says, "Hummingbird moths, that visit the lilac blossoms, are the closest we get to having hummingbirds in Fairbanks!"

Returning to the coast, the William Heaths in Kenai and Dave Delap in Anchorage feed birds the entire year, attracting many of the same species that John Leipzig has, plus several others as well. Additions include the black-billed magpie and Steller's jay, and in summer, pine siskins, dark-eyed juncos, white-crowned and fox sparrows. Feeders are supplied with sunflower, white proso millet, niger, suet, and table scraps.

Feeding Eagles

Anchorage and Kenai are located on the south coast of Alaska on Cook Inlet, west of the Alaska panhandle. Seventy miles south of Kenai on Cook Inlet is Alaska's best-known bird feeding operation. In 1979, Jean Keene, who works at a fish processing plant, began tossing out leftover seafood scraps in winter to bald eagles that frequented the coast near her home at the Homer Spit. Besides enjoying having the spectacular birds

North America's largest concentration of bald eagles is found in Alaska.

nearby, she wanted to help immature eagles get through their first winter and to assist in rehabilitating injured eagles. From a small beginning her program grew in scope every year until she is now playing host to almost 400 eagles a day. After obtaining the food at the processing plant, Ms. Keene transports it to her home, where she cuts up the scrap shrimp, crab, and fish, throwing it out, piece by piece every morning, to the congregated eagles. Gulls by the hundreds (mostly glaucous-winged gulls) wait patiently to get a bite, as do many northwestern crows.

The eagles hold their own and steal the show, which attracts hundreds of human visitors as well. But the bird watchers must stay in their cars; otherwise the eagles will become alarmed and fly away. They seem to trust only their hostess.

Year-Round Blossoms for Hummingbirds

Jeanette Urbain in Seattle has carefully picked hummingbird plants that will do well in her small yard and provide a steady succession of blossoms throughout the year. In late February, her flowering quince (*Chaenomeles*) produces red blossoms that are eagerly visited by her Anna's hummingbirds. A little later, the Anna's and early-arriving rufous hummingbirds turn to her red-flowering currant bushes. The rufous hummingbirds tend to time their return to northern nesting grounds to the opening of the currant blossoms. Early spring also sees coralbells coming into bloom. Ms. Urbain lines her flower beds with these plants and also uses them as ground cover.

The penstemons in her yard, with their tubular pink, white, or purple flowers, come into bloom by early summer and produce blossoms well into the fall. Summer speedwells (*Veronica*), bee balm, and tritonia (*Montbretia*) are still other flowers she maintains which are patronized by the Anna's through the summer. Two mints—lion's-ear (*Leonotis leonurus*) and germander (*Teucrium*)—provide a succession of blossoms through the summer into late fall. By late summer her rosemary, with its small blue flowers and fragrant foliage, is having a second blooming season. Both bees and hummingbirds favor its spring and fall blossoms.

Pineapple sage, a popular hummingbird plant in both the Southwest and California, is one of Ms. Urbain's favorites. She says the hummingbirds are so eager to obtain the nectar that they begin probing the flower buds before they are open. The blooming season lasts from August until mid-December. With the help of pineapple sage, penstemon, and germander, hum-

*The sphinx moth
is sometimes
mistaken for a
hummingbird.
Both bird and
moth drink nectar
from flowers.*

mingbirds have blossoms to visit at least through early winter. Supplementing these flowers are fuchsia blossoms on plants that Ms. Urbain brings indoors on cold days and puts out again when the weather warms.

Add winter-blooming camellias and jasmine to Ms. Urbain's list and it can be seen that the Pacific Northwest as far north as Vancouver has enough flowers in winter to supplement the sugar water diet that the Anna's hummingbirds rely upon. By early spring, there is such a profusion of blossoms and small flying insects that the birds are capable of becoming much more independent.

Food Plants for Other Birds

Most of the temperate zone bird food plants that we have already met do well under the moist, mild conditions of the coastal Northwest. There are other new ones that have been introduced from far-flung parts of the world, such as New Zealand and Chile. As in California, only a botanist can identify the many native and introduced plants growing in parks and gardens from Vancouver southward. Here, as in other mild parts of North America, the dogwoods, hollies, honeysuckles, viburnums, crabapples, mountain ashes, cotoneasters, pyracantha, and nandina are widely planted. Not to be overlooked are the apple trees so widely planted for their fruit in the coastal belt. Birds feed on fallen and overly ripe fruit through the fall and into winter.

Many native trees and shrubs that furnish food for birds in California are also present in much of the Pacific Northwest. Mention has already been made of the elderberries, madrone, and Oregon grape, the latter being the state flower of Oregon. Other native plants bearing fruits well-liked by birds include Pacific dogwood, red-osier dogwood, wild cherries, and Pacific wax myrtle. Ornamentals with good bird-attracting properties are the huckleberries (*Vaccinium*). Writing of the part these plants and the mountain ash play, E.A. Kitchins, in his *Birds of the Olympic Peninsula*, states:

"The greatest autumnal feast of all is held on the high huckleberry and mountain ash slopes. The ripening fruit attracts birds by the hundreds. Band-tailed pigeons in large flocks come to gorge upon the huckleberries. Joining them are robins, flickers, bluebirds, thrushes, and sparrows. The sooty [blue] grouse, their crops distended, hate even to fly. The fermenting juice of the berries has a hilarious effect on many of the birds. Then come the red mountain ash berries that last until the leaves fall and the bushes are bare."

Special Problems

A problem in the rainy season is that bird food becomes moldy in feeders or on the ground. Poor sanitation and moldy food, as discussed in Chapter 13, can lead to several bird diseases. But by taking proper precautions, feeder operators can safeguard the health of their charges. Jeanette Urbain of Seattle advises that feeders be cleaned almost daily in wet weather. She also points out that the wood in wooden feeders absorbs moisture and that this can affect the food in the feeder. Well-made tubular hanging feeders and those with a tray and adjustable plastic dome are the best ones to use in a wet climate. In wet weather very little food should be placed on the ground—as a rule, no more than birds can eat in a day. □

Chapter 12

BIRD FEEDING SURVEYS

Surveys of feeding station operators provided valuable information for this book.

It is not surprising that people who feed birds are being asked to participate in surveys of various kinds. The suppliers of bird food and bird feeders, for example, want to know how well their products are being received. They have many questions: How much of a demand is there for squirrel-proofing? How many people feed hummingbirds and how well do their hummingbird feeders work? Is there any need for red food coloring or fortified sugar solutions? It is not generally realized that a big industry supplies the needs of some 90 million persons who feed birds in the U.S.

and Canada. More than $1 billion a year is spent on bird food alone in the United States. Moreover, bird watching is the second most popular outdoor pastime in North America, second only to gardening.

Besides helping to create better products, surveys provide answers to questions asked by those who do the feeding (see Chapter 13). Many of those who feed birds wonder if the trends they see at their feeders are widespread or not. They want to share what they see with others. They wonder if the unusual bird or bird behavior they see at their feeders is worth getting excited about. And what about the poor season when far fewer birds than normal show up? Scarcity awakens worries about pesticides, acid rain, the cutting of tropical rain forests, and the prospects of a "silent spring."

State feeder surveys, such as those referred to in Chapter 4, provide information on species and numbers at feeders during specified times of the year. These surveys are often a part of nongame programs conducted by state wildlife conservation departments. They provide information on overall population trends of wintering birds. This kind of information is not only of interest to those who feed birds, but it helps the wildlife departments determine which species' populations are increasing, which are constant, and which are decreasing and may need help. If classified as endangered or threatened, the species may be eligible for special help in the form of habitat preservation, or direct efforts such as special plantings or the erection of nest boxes. Bluebirds furnish a good example of this type of program. The widescale distribution of bluebird nest boxes along roadways and special bluebird trails has revived bluebird populations throughout North America.

A winter bird feeder survey conducted by the Long Point Bird Observatory in Ontario was the first privately operated survey of this kind. Initiated in 1971, the program has provided information on long-term population trends among feeder birds in Ontario. Its coordinator, Erica Dunn, has expanded these efforts over the years into a continentwide survey of feeder bird populations.

In 1987, the Cornell Laboratory of Ornithology in cooperation with the Long Point Bird Observatory began its Project FeederWatch. With 4,000 participants in 1987-88, the program was off to a good start. The aim of FeederWatch was to learn more about our feeder birds, their species and numbers, and to monitor changes in their distribution and abundance. By 1990 the program had 8,000 participants and was represented in all of the mainland states of the United States and all the provinces of Canada. About one fourth of the participants live in the western half of the continent. Project FeederWatch hopes to attain a total membership of approximately 15,000. (To become a Feeder-Watch participant, write to the Cornell Laboratory of Ornithology, 159 Sapsucker Woods Road, Ithaca, New York 14850.)

Persons who feed birds are also invited to participate in programs that are not ongoing but which seek answers to specific questions. For example, Margaret Brittingham, whose studies I report upon in the following two chapters, was interested in finding out how widespread certain avian diseases are among feeder birds. Using the state of Wisconsin as her sample area, she and her associate in this study sent questionnaires to a large number of persons who fed birds. The 624 responses from households in the state were highly useful in helping the researchers evaluate the seriousness of the problem.

I am among those who have used questionnaires to obtain information on bird feeding and related matters. Both Audubon Workshop of Northbrook, Illinois, and *Bird Watcher's Digest* have cooperated in these ventures. The Workshop survey was in connection with my book *Summer Bird Feeding*. A *Bird Watcher's Digest* questionnaire sent to people who feed birds in the West yielded more than 100 responses that helped provide information for this book. An earlier *BWD* questionnaire helped Pat Murphy and me obtain information for two *BWD* articles on feeding and attracting hummingbirds.

Where Are the Birds?

For those who do most of their bird feeding from midfall until midspring, the perennial question at the start of the season is: "Where are the birds?" In early fall, when natural food is most abundant, birds are busy foraging elsewhere. It usually takes a combination of bad weather and natural food shortage to bring birds to our feeders. If there is no pressing reason for them to come, they may delay their appearance or not appear at all.

A second reason for a poor season at our feeders is the failure of northern finches to put in an appearance. As with our usual visitors, this may be a matter of plentiful natural food supplies and mild weather. If conditions favor over-wintering in the north, the finches may have no reason to travel southward.

The scenarios I have outlined, however, should not be taken too literally. There are always some birds that dutifully turn up at feeders regardless of the weather and natural food supplies. It would be an unusual winter indeed if dark-eyed juncos and house sparrows did not appear. FeederWatch surveys conducted from 1987 through early 1990 found the dark-eyed junco to be the most widely reported feeder species throughout the continent. These same surveys revealed the house sparrow to be the most abundant feeder species, even though it visited fewer feeders than the juncos. According to FeederWatch, other widespread species likely to be seen every year include the mourning dove, blue jay, northern cardinal, house finch, and American goldfinch. In Canada, the black-capped chickadee is the most common and widespread bird at feeders.

In its initial survey (feeder counts from November, 1987, through March, 1988) FeederWatch registered what might be called an "average" year. A relatively slow pace at many feeders was overshadowed by a spectacular invasion of pine siskins. Millions of the small birds streamed southward, appearing at feeding stations in greater numbers than had been seen in years. Failure of the natural seed harvest within the breeding range was given as the probable cause for the irruption.

If the 1987-88 season seemed a bit disappointing, what were FeederWatch participants to say about the next year? Nearly all species were present in below-average numbers, as was reported in *FeederWatch News*: "Decreases occurred across the entire winter range of some species, such as northern cardinal, purple finch, pygmy nuthatch, mountain chickadee, and white-throated and white-crowned sparrows."

The scrub jay showed a marked drop in numbers on the

Surveys also help to monitor "boom and bust" species, such as pine siskins.

West Coast and the red-breasted nuthatch in the Northwest. The pine siskin appeared at only half as many feeders as the previous year, not unexpected for a bird that is considered a "boom or bust" species. A plentiful harvest of tree seeds in the North seemed responsible for the decline in this species and several other birds as well.

FeederWatch results for its third year (1989-90) did a lot to allay the fears of those who had begun to suspect a decrease in songbirds and feeder birds. The pine siskins were back again, in numbers comparable to those of the first year. *FeederWatch News* reported that nearly every bird species that is common at feeders visited them in higher numbers in January, 1990, than in January, 1989. The biggest gainers were the American goldfinch, purple finch, and pine siskin. Sparrows were another group that gained—among them dark-eyed juncos, chipping sparrows, American tree sparrows, Harris' sparrows, and white-crowned sparrows. But a sparrow of a different sort, the house sparrow, did not show an increase, for which many were grateful. Oddly, house sparrows were found to appear in greatest numbers early in the winter season and thereafter to begin to decline.

Western Feeder Survey

In 1989, *Bird Watcher's Digest* initiated a small-scale survey directed to persons who feed birds in the West. Information was obtained through questionnaires and correspondence with about 200 feeder operators in the eight regions treated in this book. [For purposes of reporting these results, I have combined the eastern and western Great Plains into one Great Plains region. Project FeederWatch also uses a regional approach, but its western regions have different names and boundaries than those reported here.]

As in the Project FeederWatch survey, the house sparrow and dark-eyed junco were among the most common and widespread visitors to bird feeders. This was true even though the *BWD* survey covered the entire year whereas FeederWatch limits its survey to the November-to-April period.

On a year-round basis, the dark-eyed junco was the most widespread feeder bird only in the Pacific Northwest. Elsewhere, except in the Rockies and Far North, it was largely a winter visitor. With the exception of the Pacific Northwest (where it ranked third), the house sparrow was the second most common feeder bird. The house finch, rapidly spreading throughout much of North America, held first place as the most widespread feeder bird in the Southwest, the Rockies, and California. In the northern Great Plains region, black-capped chickadees were the most common and widespread feeder birds; the Carolina chickadee held this distinction in southern Great Plains. The Inca dove held first place in South Texas.

Comparing Survey Participants

The Spring, 1989, issue of *FeederWatch News* provides a profile of the survey's average participant, and supplies information on the typical feeding station. [This was for the 1988-1989 season when Project FeederWatch had more than 7,000 participants in the U.S. and Canada.]

Coordinator Erica Dunn writes:

"The average FeederWatcher lived in a small town, in a detached house more than 10 years old located less than 100 yards from its neighbors. Both deciduous and evergreen trees grew near the feeders, and there were woods and open areas within a half-mile of the house. The majority of feeder sites were regularly disturbed by cats, dogs, and especially by people."

Writing about numbers and kinds of bird feeders, she reported that more than three-quarters of all FeederWatchers had six or seven feeders, including at least one suet feeder, one platform feeder, and more than one hanging feeder. Hummingbird feeders were present in 75 percent of the yards on the West Coast. In Alaska, only 50 percent of feeder operators threw seed on the ground, probably since it is covered quickly by snow. In contrast, 96 percent of those participating in Texas and Oklahoma scattered seed on the ground. Water, so important to birds everywhere, especially in drier parts of the West, was provided regularly by 57 percent of FeederWatchers. More than 80 percent of those feeding birds on the West Coast supplied water.

The *Bird Watcher's Digest* survey asked for information on the number of years participants had been feeding birds, seasons when feeding was conducted, and the kind of area (urban, suburban, rural) where the participant lived. The number of years that participants had been feeding birds showed what a hold this pursuit has upon those who take it up. The average number of years that participants in California had been feeding birds was 15 years. Norm and Maggie Mellor of Corona, California, helped boost the average by having fed birds for 42 years. In Washington the average was even higher, at 19 years.

With only one exception, year-round feeding was the rule in California, where, as already noted, hummingbird feeding is also a year-round activity. Year-round feeding was not as widely practiced in other parts of the West. Seventy-five percent or more of the participants in the Southwest and South Texas fed birds the entire year, but only 50 percent in the Great Plains region. Those who did not feed birds throughout the year, for the most part confined their feeding to fall, winter, and spring.

BWD survey participants were as follows: 20 percent lived in urban areas, 50 percent in the suburbs, and 30 percent in rural areas. Under the heading of nuisance mammals, the house cat led by far in every region, squirrels were the next most unpopular mammal, and there were relatively few complaints about any other four-footed beasts. In California, where anti-cat sentiment was especially strong, the house cat received a disapproval rating of 54 percent in the *BWD* survey. Squirrels of several species were also unpopular among many who feed birds, and received a disapproval rating of 23 percent.

Unwelcome Birds

A topic not covered by FeederWatch is that of unwelcome birds at bird feeders. This happens to be one of the most controversial subjects related to feeding birds. The bird that may be welcomed at one feeder may be in disfavor at another. Almost any bird, if it arrives in large numbers and eats too much, may lose favor. This can happen with birds as interesting and colorful as the jays and the evening grosbeak. The *BWD* survey showed the house sparrow to be by far the most unpopular feeder bird in

Predators, such as this accipiter, are a natural element of feeder birds' lives.

every region. In the Great Plains, where it is particularly abundant, it had a disapproval rating of 41 percent. In fact, it was found to have about the same rating among birds that the house cat has among mammals.

The domestic pigeon, or rock dove, and the European starling, which have many of the same faults as the house sparrow, fared somewhat better. The pigeon is a bird of city parks and the starling is usually a bad weather bird at feeders, its diet largely limited to suet and softer foods. The hawks, including the small accipiters, fared quite well. Although some of those whose feeders were visited by hawks deplored losses inflicted upon feeder birds, most had the philosophy that "hawks have to eat too." A Californian, who felt this way, added, "It's quite a thrill to have a Cooper's or sharp-shinned hawk swoop at the feeders."

There were complaints about the common grackle in the Great Plains region, the Inca dove in South Texas, and cowbirds in the Southwest, Rockies, and California.

The nuisance birds had their defenders as well as critics. For example, Ella Jones of Aurora, Colorado, writes, "We enjoy the occasional blue jays that come to our feeders. We love the house finches, and tolerate the house sparrows." Virgil J. Ketner of Ventura, California, is even more outspoken on the subject. He writes, "Only Easterners consider some species 'bad'. We like them all." But he admits to having a problem keeping starlings from usurping his flicker house. In Chapter 13, I have more to say about so-called problem birds and our attitudes regarding them.

Feeders

The *BWD* and FeederWatch surveys obtained closely similar results regarding kinds of feeders used and how seed is used. Both surveys indicated that in all regions respondents fed birds at multiple feeders and that platform and hanging tubular feeders were equally popular. Nearly everyone also had at least one feeder for suet or suet mixes. Thistle feeders and special feeders to hold fruit were less widely used. A surprising finding was that nearly everyone offered food on the ground as well as at raised feeders. In some cases, participants said that enough food fell from raised feeders to supply the needs of dominantly ground-feeding birds.

There was an awareness on the part of many that ground feeding had its risks. One was that birds feeding on the ground are more vulnerable to being preyed upon by house cats; another was that food is more likely to spoil on the ground and may also become contaminated by bird droppings. Conrad and Martha Wiederhold of Frazier Park, California, say their soil is sandy and dry and that they regularly change the locations where food is scattered. In this way they reduce the danger to birds from feeder-related diseases. We will return to this topic in the next chapter.

Seeds and Other Foods

Regarding bird foods, both surveys show that sunflower is the most commonly offered food at bird feeders everywhere in the West. One hundred percent of FeederWatch participants in the northern Great Plains and Idaho supplied sunflower at their feeders and 97 to 99 percent nearly everywhere else. The *BWD* survey showed that of the sunflower seeds, black oil was by far the most common variety used and that shelled sunflower or sunflower meats were preferred over unshelled by a small number of participants.

In both surveys millet alone, or mixed bird seeds containing millet, ranked next to sunflower in popularity. White proso millet was considered superior to other millets for bird feeding. Other ingredients in mixtures, such as milo, cracked corn, cracked wheat, flax seeds, and canary seeds, received better reports in some regions than in others. Milo was rated highly by those who use it in warmer parts of the West, but not so highly in the more northern sections. Cracked corn was given a similar rating. Niger, generally offered separately in hanging feeders, was popular in the eastern Great Plains region, where it was used by 89 percent of FeederWatch participants. Elsewhere in the West, niger was less popular, with only a 32 percent usage in the West Coast region and 13 percent in Alaska. Safflower seeds, according to FeederWatch, are becoming more popular with feeder owners and feeder visitors alike. One of the advantages of safflower seeds is that they are not overly attractive to grackles and other less desirable visitors. Suet and suet mixes were widely used, and were about equally popular among users in all regions. Meat scraps, with their high protein content and strong appeal to more northerly birds, were popular in Alaska and the northern Great Plains region. Bread, as well as other bakery products, and fruit were widely used but not to the extent of most other foods. The only region where fruit was not used was Alaska.

Turning to the *BWD* survey, which asked for food uses

throughout the year, it was not unexpected to find that sugar water was widely used. One hundred percent of those who fed birds in South Texas and California supplied sugar water and almost the same percentage in all other regions except the Great Plains, where hummingbirds are much less common. Many of those who feed birds in the West take up bird feeding because of hummingbirds and only later begin feeding other birds as well.

Surveys show that black oil sunflower, white proso millet, and thistle are the most popular seeds.

Water

There is one ingredient that all birds need: water. Most people who feed birds recognize this and have one or more bird baths. *FeederWatch News* reported that more than 80 percent of those who fed birds in southern areas and on the West Coast supplied water. The *BWD* survey, with its smaller samples, obtained even higher percentages for roughly the same regions. One hundred percent of those who responded in South Texas and California supplied water and 90 percent of those in the Southwest. Northward, where there is greater rainfall, the number of those having birdbaths was not as great—75 percent in the Pacific Northwest and less than 50 percent in the Great Plains region. Some of those who did not have birdbaths said there was no need to since they lived close to ponds or streams.

Other Observations

In the *BWD* questionnaire space was left for additional comments, which I always look forward to reading. Jewel A. Gifford of Springdale, Utah, told about a sharp-shinned hawk that met its match when it flew into the enclosure where she kept her bantam chickens. The hawk had been turned over on its back by an angry hen and was getting such a thorough drubbing that she had to rescue it. She kept the badly battered hawk in a container overnight and released it the next morning. She said it was "soon back in business as usual," and added, "What a relief! I'd have hated to admit to anyone that one of my bantam hens had killed a hawk!"

The Norm Mellors in California stated that they never have to spray their roses with insecticide because of services rendered by Bewick's wrens and warblers.

More than enough odd tastes can be observed at the feeding station. Examples from *FeederWatch News* include red-headed woodpeckers eating oyster crackers, robins eating raisin bread and cooked sweet potato, and a long list of birds eating pet foods such as dog chow, cat kibble, and rabbit pellets. Someone even thought of mixing baked beans and peanut butter and offering it at the feeder. The concoction was said to be wildly successful!

There is no end to the observations that can be made when feeding birds. That is why it is so important to have a pencil and notebook handy to record interesting bird behavior when watching at the window. Bird behavior is not stereotypical. Birds are always up to something unusual. □

Chapter 13

QUESTIONS PEOPLE ASK

Bird behavior probably generates more curiosity among humans than does any other aspect of the natural world.

B egin-
ning in 1982,
Bird Watcher's Digest
instituted a new column called "The Backyard Bird
Watcher's Question Box." Over the years, this column has provided answers to hundreds of questions sent in from all over
North America. Easily one-fourth of the questions pertain to bird
feeding. Judging from the kind of bird feeding questions the
column receives, the greatest interest centers around (1) foods to
use, (2) dangers of mortality at feeders, (3) competition at feeders, and (4) the best ways to feed hummingbirds.

This chapter is filled with answers to the most frequently
asked questions about bird feeding. They are drawn from material published by *Bird Watcher's Digest* since the debut of the

"Question Box." In some cases answers are supplemented by my own experience and observations. Undoubtedly these questions will generate other questions you may have about bird feeding. When you find you can't answer the question yourself, send it to "The Backyard Bird Watcher's Question Box." *BWD*, P.O. Box 110, Marietta, Ohio 45750.

Q: What is the best type of birdseed to offer?

A: Sunflower seed, whether the black oil or striped variety, is one of the most nutritious and popular foods we can offer birds. The seeds are excellent sources of protein, calcium, phosphorus, potassium, carbohydrates, and vitamins. Good for year-round bird feeding, whether in the hot Southwest or cooler Pacific Northwest, sunflower has become the standard food that nearly everyone uses. The trend is toward black oil sunflower seed over striped because of its higher nutritional value. In the smaller black oil type, 70 percent of the seed is meat in contrast to only 57 percent in striped sunflower. In addition, black oil seed has a softer shell more easily opened by small birds.

For those who would rather not be bothered with the litter that comes from discarded shells left by birds, there is the option of buying sunflower meats. Some claim that the meats bring even more species to the feeder and, in the long run, can be more economical than sunflower that is unshelled.

Compared to sunflower, thistle (niger) seed is a newcomer to the bird food market. Long used as a food for caged birds, it was only 15 years ago that this import from Ethiopia and India began to be used extensively as a food at bird feeders. It is an ideal food for pine siskins, goldfinches, redpolls, and other small finches and has the advantage of not inviting squirrels and most larger birds. Even mourning doves will peck at and eat seeds that fall to the ground, a guarantee that none of the seeds will be wasted. Thistle should always be offered in hanging feeders that are especially designed to hold seeds this small. If the seeds are not consumed within a week or more, they may begin to become rancid and unpalatable. A sure sign of this is a thistle feeder with a long-standing residue of uneaten seeds in it.

Q: Is there a risk of causing a disease if I don't clean my feeders? What happens if I don't detect and discard moldy seed in time?

A: One cannot emphasize too strongly the importance of

freshness in the seeds and grains of all kinds used for bird feeding. As I stated in my book *Summer Bird Feeding*: "Seeds that are rancid, moldy, or worm-infested are poorer in vitamins, protein, and other nutrients than fresh seeds. If rancid or moldy, the seed could represent a health hazard to birds."

Seeds having a high oil content have a tendency to become rancid in hot weather, and therefore special precautions should be taken with high-oil seeds such as sunflower, thistle, safflower, and peanuts. Where the climate is very hot, buy only small amounts of any of these foods at a time and, if practicable, store in a refrigerator or freezer. Place only as much food in bird feeders as birds can quickly eat. The most likely place for a food to become moldy and unfit for consumption is at the bottom of a bird feeder!

Q: **Is peanut butter safe for birds?**

A: The controversy over peanut butter all began in 1961, when Charles Nichols, a biologist at the American Museum of Natural History, autopsied several black-capped chickadees that he found dead at his feeders and discovered that their esophagi were clogged with peanut butter. Against this inconclusive evidence, many people have cited examples of birds living to old age that have had extended access to peanut butter. I found much the same thing when, years ago, I was feeding birds peanut butter and banding them to determine, among other things, their longevity.

To condemn a food on the basis of a few examples of possible harmful effect seems unjustified. Many of the foods that birds eat in the wild are potentially much more dangerous than anything we offer at the feeder. Birds choke while eating some wild foods; others cause inebriation or have toxic effects (see pages 746-747 in John K. Terres' *Encyclopedia of North American Birds*.) The peanut butter argument can best be summed up by saying that chances of birds being harmed by eating it are minimal and that peanut butter is perhaps best used in mixtures such as the ones already described.

Q: **Is it true that birds will die if they eat uncooked rice?**

A: This question has been asked often by people wanting to know about possible dangers to birds if they eat uncooked rice, such as that tossed at weddings. From research done on the properties of rice, we have learned that wheat and rice expand to about the same degree when exposed to moisture and that neither could possibly harm a bird by expanding after it was ingested. Although not commonly used in bird feeding, rice does have a few takers. Marian Pennington of Pico Rivera, California, reports that hundreds of birds eat rice in her backyard with no ill effect. Among them are mourning doves, spotted doves, scrub jays, and house sparrows.

Q: Is suet safe for birds in summer?

A: Suet is the one food that meets the needs of seed-eating and insectivorous birds alike, and therefore should be included in our bird food menu. A drawback is the tendency of suet to melt or spoil in hot weather. One specific worry is that melted suet can cause matting of breast feathers in woodpeckers which are especially fond of this food.

There are a number of ways to overcome these problems. If possible, use kidney suet. It is firm, hard, and not as prone to melting. But by far the best way to offer suet is to render it over slow heat until completely melted. Rendering removes impurities and moisture and thereby produces a form of suet that is much more resistant to melting and spoilage. But having gone to this trouble, one might as well add a few ingredients that will further reduce chances of melting, creating an even more nutritious and inviting food for birds. Of the many recipes that can be used, the following is as good as any:

Hairy woodpecker on suet.

Mix together the following ingredients:
1 cup melted suet
1 cup of melted peanut butter
4 cups of cornmeal (white or yellow)
1 cup of white flour

Place in a mold and allow to harden. Birds will devour this mixture even more readily than suet.

John K. Terres, in his book *Songbirds in Your Garden*, recommends this recipe but uses vegetable shortening instead of melted suet. His "Marvel Meal," as he calls it, is well-suited for use in either hot or cold weather.

Another way to get around the melting problem is to bring the suet or suet mixture indoors at night, or even during the hottest part of the day, placing it in the freezer. This treatment will reduce chances of melting and, if indoors at night, the suet won't be subject to possible theft by marauding nocturnal mammals. For those who feed birds in the mountains, it is advisable to fasten down suet securely; otherwise large birds, like nutcrackers and gray jays, will remove the suet, feeder and all!

Whatever method is used to make use of suet, it should be remembered that suet is one of the most nutritional foods to offer young birds recently out of the nest. The clamoring and goings-on that take place when parents bring their young to the suet are among the best shows of the year!

Q: Are the prepackaged seed mixes good to offer at my feeders?

A: Many feeder operators question the value of the seeds and ingredients in birdseed mixtures. The best advice is to buy each seed type separately and find out for oneself. Many birdseed buyers complain that milo and some of the other ingredients in mixtures sold at supermarkets are not eaten. Milo, a variety of sorghum, is an inexpensive grain widely grown in the Southwest which sometimes, along with millet and cracked corn, makes up the largest share of the mixture.

In the March/April 1988 issue of *Bird Watcher's Digest*, Ralph A. Fisher, Jr. of Silver City, New Mexico strongly defended milo and said that the complaints of eastern writers were "a lot of malarkey!" I also came to the defense of milo in a later issue (September/October 1989). If milo is harvested at the right stage and isn't a bitter variety that is grown for the sole purpose of repelling birds that come to the sorghum fields, it is as popular with ground-feeding birds as any other food. In the Southwest, where there are proportionally more doves, gallinaceous birds, blackbirds, and jays than in the East, milo is one of the most commonly used foods in bird feeding. But nothing would induce the chickadees, titmice, nuthatches, and other tree foragers, so common in the East, to eat milo.

Some seed companies now produce mixtures with specific bird species or regional seed preferences in mind. These "gourmet" mixes are more expensive but attract proportionally more birds and leave fewer uneaten seeds at our feeders.

Q: What should I offer birds that feed on the ground?

A: Food for ground-feeding birds should be offered on the ground, and this includes milo, any of the several millets, canary seed, cracked corn, buckwheat, and rape. Alternatively, the food can be offered on shelves and bird tables or platform feeders, but not in hanging feeders. These should be reserved for sunflower and thistle.

Q: Is there some way I can keep the blackbirds and doves from dominating my feeders?

A: Birds of every feather come thronging to the feeders when snow covers their natural food supply. At such times we can afford to waste some of the less expensive food by throwing it out onto packed snow where it will distract field-foragers from going to hanging feeders.

Q: Where is the best place to buy birdseed?

A: One of the best places is a feed store that sells to farmers and gardeners. The food at such outlets is almost always fresh and can be purchased in bulk, which is much less expensive. Another source that I can recommend are stores that specialize in products related to feeding and attracting birds. Many have mail-order catalogues and will ship seed to customers wherever they may be. Still another source of bird food are the birdseed sales, such as the annual "Birdseed Savings Day," conducted by many local bird clubs. Many offer birdseed at special discount prices.

Birdless feeders are nothing to be alarmed about.

Q: Why are there no birds at my feeder? I keep them clean, put out the foods they like, and see no cats or hawks nearby.

A: There is an ever present tug between natural food supplies

and food supplied at our feeders. Even when feeder foods seem in greater demand, birds continue to obtain most of their food in the wild. Only during emergencies are birds likely to become dependent upon the feeder for most of their food. When natural food is most plentiful (usually late summer until late fall) feeders may be almost entirely abandoned. But birds always return when their wild food supply begins to dwindle.

Feeders also may be deserted when a small hawk, such as a sharp-shinned hawk, Cooper's hawk, or kestrel, takes up residence in the neighborhood. Generally these appearances are short-lived, and our feeder birds can adjust to their presence by dashing out from cover, feeding, and quickly returning. Some birds, such as cardinals, several of the sparrows, and juncos, time visits to pre-dawn and dusk hours when darkness helps conceal them from the eyes of predators.

Q: Are feeders themselves ever to blame for poor attendance?

A: Sometimes this may be the case. Many manufacturers, in responding to complaints about squirrels and so-called nuisance birds, have produced such impregnable fortresses that even agile chickadees can scarcely gain entrance! Food should be plainly in view and reasonably easy for birds to reach. Best results will be obtained with a variety of feeders and foods.

Q: Occasionally I find a dead bird at my feeders. What causes this?

A: Mortality at feeders is fairly commonplace. The survival rates of most bird species are less than 50 percent from the time of leaving the nest until the following spring, so no one should be unduly alarmed by the occasional discovery of a dead bird in the yard. But if the fault is ours, it should prompt us to do something about it. The two biggest causes of death at our feeders are avian diseases and window strikes (see question below). Losses from both can be greatly reduced if only a few precautions are taken.

Some of the best advice for controlling avian diseases came from one of the "Question Box" correspondents, Jeane Florence of Herndon, Virginia, who has never had a problem with birds contracting disease. She writes: "We use tube feeders and other hanging feeders that do not allow birds to sit on their food supply and contaminate it with their feces. We feed ground-feeding birds on sills and on the patio, areas that can easily be kept clean through a once-a-week scrubbing with soap and a disinfectant. People who feed directly on the ground can rotate areas over periods of several days, or the areas can be cleaned with a splash of boiling water."

To prevent avian pox, a particularly difficult disease to control, a five percent bleach solution was recommended for cleaning feeders.

A study by Margaret Clark Brittingham and Stanley A. Temple, conducted in Wisconsin and published in a 1988 issue of *The Passenger Pigeon*, provides detailed information on diseases associated with bird feeding. The principal disease causing mortality in feeder birds was salmonellosis. This disease spreads from fecal contamination of food eaten at or near the feeder. Infected birds often have diarrhea and become weak and listless before they die.

A second disease, trichomoniasis, primarily affects pigeons and doves and is caused by a parasite that lodges in the bird's throat and lungs. The disease is spread by way of other birds eating food dropped from the mouth of an infected bird.

Coccidiosis, which is especially prevalent in house sparrows, is spread by birds eating food that has been contaminated by feces. Victims of the disease have diarrhea, become weak, and occasionally die.

Still another disease, aspergillosis, is caused by a fungus found in damp or wet bird food. Birds breathing in the spores may die from bronchitis or pneumonia. This is a disease that is most prevalent in damp climates. Avian pox, sometimes called foot pox, is especially common in house finches. The visible signs are warty lesions on the feet and head. Afflicted birds may survive but are at a disadvantage.

Q: There is a bald cardinal at my feeder. Is this a normal part of the molting process?

A: Tiny mites cause a disease called avian mange, the primary symptom of which is feather loss. So-called "bald birds" that have lost the feathers on the top of their head probably have this affliction. It is spread from one bird to another by crowding, such as at our feeders.

In spite of the formidable array of diseases that can be spread by birds at feeders, Brittingham and Temple, on analyzing questionnaire returns from 624 households in Wisconsin where birds were fed, found that only 16 percent of the respondents had observed at least one occurrence of mortality due to disease or unknown causes. The house sparrow was by far the most frequent victim of disease. Seven times as many dead or dying house sparrows were found than the next most frequently involved species, which was the American goldfinch. Only gregarious species were afflicted by disease. Besides the two species already mentioned, dark-eyed juncos, mourning doves, evening grosbeaks, and common grackles were affected to some degree.

A significant finding was that mortality occurred more often at platform feeders, rather than on other types of feeders. This, in the words of the researchers, was because at these feeders birds stand in the food, and this increases the probability of contamination by fecal matter. Good reason to wash, scrub, and offer birds only the amount of food that can quickly be eaten!

Q: How can I keep birds from flying into my windows?

A: This is one of the most worrisome problems connected with bird feeding. Sometimes the birds are killed, but more often they are badly injured or stunned. Certain windows in a house are always more subject to bird strikes than others, primarily because they reflect images of surrounding habitat that to the birds look like a place to alight, or like an opening through which the bird can fly. Bird feeders draw more birds to the vicinity of our houses, therefore increasing the chances for bird strikes at nearby windows. Surprisingly, window feeders are not a hazard. By feeding close to windows birds learn that the glass is not an opening.

Anything that announces the fact that the glass is a hard surface will reduce or eliminate the incidence of window strikes. A standard solution is to fasten a decal or silhouette of a diving hawk or some other predator on the inside of the window. There is some question about whether these silhouettes are effective because they actually scare birds, or because they call attention to the glass. The important thing is that they work to prevent bird strikes.

Another solution that seems to be effective and that doesn't mar our vision is fine nylon mesh netting placed against the outside edge of the glass. This solution comes from Carl Haussman of Lansing, Michigan, who says the nylon mesh is inexpensive, long-lasting, and doesn't significantly interfere with the view. It can be found at garden and farm supply stores.

Q: **What should I do with an injured bird?**

Hanging hawk or owl silhouettes may reduce window strikes. Another solution may be moving the feeders.

A: Since the handling of living, injured, or dead wild birds is prohibited by the Federal Migratory Bird Treaty Act, we are often torn between wanting to help an injured bird, and knowing it is illegal and that we may do more harm than good. When a bird flies headlong into a glass window it seems as if no small bird could withstand such a blow. But more often than not the birds that meet such an immovable object are merely stunned momentarily.

If the bird is only stunned it will quickly recover and fly away on its own. If there are cats or other pets in the vicinity and you feel you must move the bird for its safety, do so carefully. Find a safe place and move the bird, handling it as little as possible. Handling a stunned bird may cause it additional injury, trauma, or stress. In any case, a stunned bird will normally revive within an hour.

If the injured bird's condition has not improved after an hour or so, it may have internal injuries or broken bones and may be beyond help. Again, the most humane thing we can do is leave it alone, letting nature run its course. Many states have bird rehabilitation centers that you may wish to contact for advice and assistance. However, many of these centers work to help larger birds, such as hawks and owls, or endangered species. Most centers are filled to capacity, too, so their advice may be simply to leave the injured bird alone. By far the most helpful thing we can do is to make our feeders and yards safer for the birds we attract.

Q: What is the best type of bird feeder?

A: Peter Kilham, the first to design the hanging tubular feeder so common on the market today, once told me "The perfect bird feeder hasn't yet been invented." Each model has a flaw of some kind. Features I look for are durability, utility, ease of maintenance, and nice appearance.

As stated in the September 1989 issue of *Wild Bird News*, "It is false economy to buy a cheap feeder that only lasts a season or two when a better feeder can last a decade or longer. Cheaper feeders made of styrene plastic are notorious for cracking in winter, being eaten by squirrels, and shattering if dropped."

Hanging feeders of tough Lexan plastic with feeding portals reinforced with metal last for years and come closest to meeting my requirements. But, like every feeder, they require cleaning. Getting at debris that collects at the bottom of these feeders can be difficult and often requires removal of perches and loosening of screws at the bottom. The feeder should then be cleaned inside and out using warm water and a stiff long-handled brush. No matter what type of feeder you use, regular, thorough cleanings are a must.

I insist upon feeders that enhance the appearance of my yard. Fortresses to keep out squirrels, pigeons, and the like can be effective but are usually unsightly.

As far as the safety of birds is concerned, the main risk is that of contamination of food. This is good reason to keep much of the food high off the ground in tight weatherproof feeders. Some of the food, as birds feed, will spill out and fall to the ground. As long as it is quickly eaten by birds, this should not cause a health hazard. Additional food for ground-feeders can be supplied on shelf and platform feeders, and, under suitable conditions, on the ground. In dry climates it is reasonably safe to scatter food on the ground. The same is true if food is scattered on packed snow or frozen ground.

Q: How can I keep squirrels from emptying my feeders?

A: Few questions appear more often than ones about competition from squirrels. Many solutions have been tried, but the squirrel, with a tenacity unmatched by other members of the animal kingdom, always seems to win in the end. The theme has taken on almost ridiculous proportions, as seen in solutions jokingly proposed by Bill Adler, Jr. in his book *Outwitting Squirrels*. Here are a few of them:

1. Dig a moat around your feeder. Fill it with piranhas.
2. Never sleep, never play, only send out for food—and maintain a constant vigil at your feeders.
3. Bury rubber acorns—confuse and confound them.

Although squirrels for the most part live up to their reputation, they can be kept under control by resorting to a few simple measures. Donna J. P. Crossman, in the September/October 1985 issue of *Bird Watcher's Digest*, writes, "The easiest way to overcome a chronic squirrel problem is to stop thinking of it as one." For those who aren't ready to take this advice, she suggests putting out inexpensive food, such as whole shelled corn, for the squirrels. This will lure them away from the feeders.

For those who may be skeptical about this method, she has still another suggestion. Run a wire from the house to a tree in the yard and hang the bird feeder from the center of it. If the squirrels are still a problem, she writes: "You can modify the arrangement by stringing empty spools, empty film cartridges, or hose sections on the wire so that they turn freely. Any squirrel that ventures out will soon slip off."

I have been using the wire and empty cartridge method for years with complete success. It seems to work better than using the various shields, baffles, and squirrel-proof feeders. But for those who want to invest in equipment of this kind, there are plenty of products that are nearly 100 percent effective. Some even keep the birds out! It should be remembered, however, that squirrels can jump long distances from trees, rooftops, and snow banks and in this way can reach feeders that were thought to be impregnable.

*Matching wits
with squirrels can
be a frustrating
experience.
The squirrel
usually wins.*

Q: How can I discourage blackbirds? They eat so much!

A: Next to squirrels, no group is more troublesome than what can loosely be called dark-plumaged birds. Birds as unrelated to each other as crows, starlings, and grackles fall into this group. They have the distinction of having partly or wholly dark or black plumage and a reputation for being big eaters at our feeders. The dark plumage seems to conjure up superstitions that go back to the Middle Ages, when crows and ravens were associated with evil deeds and vultures were considered a sign of imminent death. Though these superstitions have little to do with our modern world, they do play a role in our attitudes toward birds and many other forms of animal life. Also important are the prejudices we may hold against introduced species. This undoubtedly influences popular thinking about the starling and house sparrow, both of which have bad reputations.

The house sparrow was unwisely introduced to cities in the East during the 1850s and the starling was released in New York City in 1890. The rapid spread of these two species since their arrival can partly be explained by their amazing ability to adapt to human habitats. Having reached peak numbers earlier this century, the house sparrow has suffered a sharp decline in numbers ever since, particularly in the East. It remains to be seen if the starling's fate will be similar.

Normally the starling does not appear at bird feeders except when snow covers its normal food supplies. It can be discouraged by limiting the foods at feeders to those it doesn't like or cannot easily consume. These include sunflower, niger, halved orange, peanuts in the shell, and a hardened suet mix (melting the suet twice and adding more cornmeal than is called for in most recipes). Foods not to offer include unrendered suet, bakery products, kitchen scraps, and finely cracked corn, all of which are readily eaten by the starling.

Other dark-plumaged birds on the not-wanted list at many feeders are harder to discourage. For a while it looked as though safflower seeds might be the answer. A white seed, about the size of sunflower and with about the same nutritive value, safflower was marketed as the perfect food for cardinals and several other finches. At the same time, early tests showed that it was not utilized by squirrels, grackles, cowbirds, and a long list of others. While this seed does not completely exclude unwanted birds, safflower does seem to be most attractive to cardinals, blue jays, and other "more desirable" feeder birds.

Starlings are voracious suet eaters.

Another solution, one already mentioned, is to offer inexpensive food well away from the center of the feeding operation. This food can be scattered on the ground or offered at platform-type feeders. Larger birds, like crows, pinyon jays, magpies, and grackles, all of which have difficulty eating at our hanging tubular feeders, can be expected to confine their feeding to the easiest source of food, which is that scattered on the ground. Admittedly some of the larger birds are skilled at fluttering before feeding portals or grasping onto a part of the feeder to obtain food. Although they may not take much, their presence scares other birds away.

Another approach is to offer as little food as possible during the time the competing birds are present. With little food present, unwanted birds may leave and not come back again. Even under these circumstances, chances are that some food can still be offered at small hanging feeders. Try putting food out very early in the morning and again near dusk, since these are periods of the day when many of the smaller birds do their feeding. These also happen to be times when the more troublesome birds are not present.

Q: Pigeons are dominating my platform feeders. What can I do?

A: The non-native, domestic pigeon, or rock dove, is as successful as the house sparrow and starling in adapting to human-made habitats. Foods not to offer when pigeons make an unwelcome appearance are corn, wheat, sorghum (milo), and bakery products. Pigeons, including our native band-tailed pigeon, as well as other members of the dove family, are fond of corn in any of its several forms. Corn can be offered elsewhere to lure these birds away from feeders, but the very presence of corn may attract other undesirable birds as well as squirrels.

Among the suggestions for discouraging pigeons are using hanging feeders with closely spaced dowels; enclosing the feeder with chicken mesh; and lowering the adjustable dome on domed feeders to exclude the larger pigeons.

For those who don't want pigeons roosting on windowsills and rooftops, here are two suggestions: Try placing wind chimes around the exterior of the house—pigeons detest the noise and will leave. Or, paint undiluted white vinegar on their roosting places!

Q: What can I do about woodpeckers drilling holes in my house?

A: Damage of this kind most often occurs to houses with redwood or cedar siding. The birds may be hearing the humming of electrical current from inside the dwellings. They interpret this as insect activity and start drilling for an easy meal. It has also been suggested that the woodpeckers use the soft wood of the siding for territorial drumming in the spring. The hollow sound the siding makes approximates their drumming on hollow tree branches and stumps. Perhaps this is a result of our not leaving adequate dead trees standing in our wooded areas.

I have been trying unsuccessfully for years to find a solution to the woodpecker damage problem. Among the suggestions I have heard are squirting the woodpeckers with water from a water pistol; covering the affected area with galvanized metal or chicken wire; and painting the area a different color (bright red or blue—non-natural wood colors). Some of these solutions seem a bit drastic, but may be resorted to by desperate homeowners.

Another method to discourage woodpeckers was suggested by Marion Dale Lag in a letter published in the September, 1990, issue of the *Nature Society News*. He writes:

"My problem birds were downy and hairy woodpeckers. They would drum on the sides of the house. Each time the birds pecked, I would bang on the inside wall exactly opposite them. Usually after two or three attempts, the birds would fly away. After several sessions of this they abandoned my home as a drilling site for at least a month. This seems almost too easy a solution, but it has worked well for me for at least 10 years."

I am sure you have many more questions than those listed here. If you can't find the answer to your bird question, send it to "The Backyard Bird Watcher's Question Box" c/o *Bird Watcher's Digest*, P.O. Box 110, Marietta, Ohio 45750. □

Chapter 14

The Benefits
of Bird Feeding

Feeding birds is educational, enjoyable, and easy to do.

Toward the end of the 19th century, bird lovers began organizing to prevent birds from being slaughtered for their feathers. What better way to interest the public in birds than to bring birds to the yard where they could be watched and studied at leisure! By giving people a backyard introduction to birds, conservationists were able to create a grassroots support that has served the cause of bird protection ever since.

By about 1915 this support had brought an end to the feather trade and had greatly slowed indiscriminate shooting. Much of the credit for getting laws passed, hiring wardens, and creating wildlife sanctuaries can be given to the National Audubon Society (then the National Association of Audubon Societies). In 1903, the first federal bird refuge was established—Pelican Island in Florida, a nesting ground for brown pelicans. Now there are more than 400 national wildlife refuges embracing some 90 million acres in Alaska, Hawaii, and the 48 states. Add to this our national parks, state wildlife refuges, Nature Conservancy and Audubon preserves, and millions of home gardens and it can be said that a great deal of progress has been made since 1900 in saving birds and other wildlife. But as the human population has grown, losses of habitat have outpaced even these conservation efforts.

Birds as Our Allies

Scientific studies of the food habits of birds have helped to promote the cause of bird protection. Before there was any factual evidence of what birds ate, many were seen as threatening various human interests, especially agricultural. It is now known that birds help control insect populations and that hawks and owls, once regarded as pests, are of invaluable service in holding down rodent populations. Indeed, the predation by small hawks and shrikes at our bird feeders provides an ecologically vital function in weeding out the weak and unfit; this helps bird populations stay healthy and alert.

Even the European starling, sometimes a nuisance when it comes to bird feeders, has redeeming traits. It consumes a long list of insect pests, including the cloverleaf weevil, ground beetle, the white grubs of the May beetle, and both larvae and adults of the Japanese beetle. E. R. Kalmbach and Ira N. Gabrielson, who conducted a study of the starling's food habits, state that, "The time the bird spends in destroying crops or molesting other birds is extremely short compared to the endless hours it spends in searching for insects and feeding on wild fruits."

There are more dramatic episodes of birds controlling an insect pest. The early Mormon settlers in Utah were twice saved from starvation by the timely arrival of gulls. In 1848 and 1855, California gulls flocked in and eradicated grasshoppers that had appeared in plague numbers and were threatening to destroy the food crops the settlers were relying upon. The appreciative Mormons erected a monument in Salt Lake City to the gulls as a tribute to their services.

On numerous other occasions crops have been saved in the West through the intervention of birds. John K. Terres, in his

A California gull with a grasshopper. This gull is Utah's state bird.

Encyclopedia of North American Birds, gives as examples meadowlarks in Washington saving crops from crickets; Brewer's blackbirds doing the same for a cankerworm infestation in California; terns, crows, and blackbirds destroying 90 percent of the white grubs exposed by plowing in Manitoba; Rocky Mountain locusts being brought under control by yellow-headed blackbirds and other blackbirds in the Great Plains; and in the same region, Franklin's gulls saving crops from grasshoppers.

Gregarious flocking species, like gulls, meadowlarks, blackbirds, and starlings, provide the most striking examples of stopping an insect plague. On the other hand, everyday feeding activities of many smaller birds—woodpeckers, chickadees, bushtits, and kinglets—keep insect pests under control without our knowing it. Birds, along with the weather and other natural agents, serve to prevent insect populations from reaching plague proportions. However, when natural controls fail it does not mean that they are not there. Rushing in with chemical solutions may produce immediate results but often at the expense of our natural allies.

Birds do much more than simply keeping down rodent and insect populations. Hummingbirds pollinate flowers; gulls, ravens, crows, and magpies act as scavengers; and birds, by their behavior, can even warn us of approaching storms. But perhaps most importantly, through their songs, bright plumage, behavior, and friendliness, birds bring us good cheer. What's more, with enjoyable activities like bird feeding, bird watching, and bird photography, we do not have to search for economic excuses to befriend them.

Does Bird Feeding Benefit Birds?

One reason that providing for birds has achieved such popularity is that both we and the bird life around us benefit. Although some people argue that birds can find all the food they need without our help, this is not always true under difficult conditions in winter. Even the hardy chickadees, which can survive harsh northern winters, may suffer greater losses in winter if they do not have feeding station foods to fall back upon.

Researchers Margaret Brittingham and Stanley A. Temple followed the life expectancy rates of black-capped chickadees in Wisconsin over a three-year period. One group of chickadees they studied had access to unlimited amounts of food at feeding stations while another sample population was isolated from the feeding stations, completely dependent upon food in the wild.

The results showed that chickadees able to obtain the extra food had a monthly survival rate of 95 percent and an over-wintering survival rate of 69 percent. On the other hand, those wholly dependent upon natural foods had a lower monthly survival rate (87 percent) and a much lower over-wintering rate (37 percent). This study showed that chickadees with access to feeders had almost twice as much chance of living through the winter as birds without this benefit.

Brittingham and Temple, who reported upon their study in an 1988 issue of *Ecology*, used mist nets to capture birds in the five study areas they established. The birds were banded, color marked with leg bands, and closely watched. During periods of very cold temperature, chickadees without access to feeders could not obtain enough food from widely dispersed natural food supplies to survive. They had to expend too much energy in their efforts to find the food, and this had to be done under conditions of short daylight hours. At the same time, plentiful supplies of food at feeders did not stop over-wintering chickadees from obtaining most of their food in the wild. Only 20 to 25 percent of their diet was composed of sunflower seed, the only food offered at feeding stations.

It is important to note that the chickadees having access to unlimited sunflower seed in this winter study did not develop a dependency on it as a food source. Once they no longer had access to this food, they were as competent as the other chickadees in the wild that hadn't been exposed to the feeding station.

The Benefits of Bird Feeding

Chickadees can hang upside down to get a sunflower seed. This type of feeder excludes larger birds such as jays and starlings.

Using our bird feeders is always a part-time occupation for birds, which have evolved over time to adapt to ever changing sources of food. It is reassuring to know that our feeding them that does not hinder their ability to obtain other foods.

Another interesting finding of this study was that sharp-shinned and Cooper's hawks, the two primary avian predators in the area, were not noticeably attracted to the concentrations of chickadees coming to the feeders. The researchers found no evidence suggesting that predation rates were higher in either case.

Brittingham and Temple compared their study to a similar one conducted in Sweden, where our black-capped chickadee has two close relatives—the crested tit and willow tit. Over-wintering survival rates of the Swedish titmice having access to supplemental feeding were 82 percent compared to only 45 percent for birds obliged to obtain all their food in the wild. Again, this showed a dramatic difference between survival chances of birds using feeders and those without this opportunity.

Although resourceful chickadees can find insect eggs and larvae even in midwinter, what about the field-foraging birds whose sources of food disappear when the ground is covered with snow? In spite of the hardships they face in winter, crows, robins, starlings, blackbirds, grackles, cowbirds, and even blue-birds often remain quite far north in winter. House sparrows, without an instinct to migrate, are obliged to do the same. David Hatch, a nature columnist for a Winnipeg newspaper, described what happened in December of 1989, when these birds, with fat reserves depleted from food scarcity, were overtaken by a mid-winter storm. Farming areas in southwestern Manitoba lost 90 percent of the resident house sparrows, and all the starlings and gray partridges. Many farms that had 100 or more house sparrows when the storm struck had none afterwards.

Other birds, too, are hard hit in severe weather. Hatch paints a bleak picture of the chances of birds such as the golden-crowned kinglet, American robin, varied thrush, white-throated sparrow, and dark-eyed junco surviving the winter. He writes:

"The keys for survival for all of these species are finding sufficient food—so that they do not have to live off their body reserves—and quality shelter from the wind. The long winter gradually wears a species down, and that is why many black-birds and other species that normally winter south of here often perish in a March blizzard or cold snap. They have no body reserves left, and when they can't secure enough food to carry them through the night, they succumb."

Ornithologist Margaret Brittingham, however, takes a somewhat different view regarding fat reserves. She writes me that small birds are capable of regaining their fat reserves quite quickly. In her studies, chickadees captured for study early in the morning have almost no body fat, but by late afternoon the same individuals have a lot of fat. She adds, "It is my impression that small birds are either in good condition for foraging or they are dead."

It is not necessary to go as far north as Wisconsin or Manitoba to find examples of heavy mortality among birds overtaken by winter storms. Anywhere in the Great Plains—even as far south as Texas, Arizona, and New Mexico—the weather can turn bad very quickly, producing losses similar to those mentioned above. This is especially true in late winter and early spring, when there is little in the way of insect or plant life to sustain birds. It is during these periods that foods at feeding stations become most important to birds.

The birds that have been with us all winter and know where the food is are the ones least likely to suffer. Foresighted woodpeckers, jays, titmice, and nuthatches store food earlier in the season. Regular feeder visitors know where to go, but early migrants, many of them insect-eaters, are the first to suffer if there is a spring snowstorm. Many of the migrants may turn to unaccustomed foods during an emergency. This is good reason to offer a wide variety of foods when winter weather suddenly returns.

Year-Round Feeding

About the time those of us in middle and northern regions of the West are putting up feeders for early arriving hummingbirds, many feeder operators are closing down feeding for other birds. I question the wisdom of doing this in my book *Summer Bird Feeding*. Not only do some of the most pleasurable and interesting periods for bird feeding lie ahead, but food takes on a new importance for birds during the nesting season. The male of a species usually has the duty of both protecting the nest and finding food. If there is not a plentiful food supply at hand, he must travel ever farther afield to obtain the insects, fruits, or berries he needs for himself and his family. In doing this, he exposes himself to greater risks than he would otherwise and uses up precious time and energy. What better help can we give birds at this season than growing food plants for them and having an adequate supply of food and water at our feeding stations?

Late spring and early summer are seasons when birds are in

their brightest plumages, bird song is at its height, and we are out-of-doors much more, better able to watch birds and follow their activities. As young birds come to feeders, accompanied by parents, we have the opportunity to view their fascinating feeding behavior.

An unusually late spring or a cool, wet early summer can result in food shortages at these seasons as well. Likely to be hardest hit are birds like swallows, swifts, and nighthawks that depend upon flying insects, and cuckoos, flycatchers, vireos, and warblers that are also highly insectivorous. Indeed, most seed-eating birds will shift to a largely insectivorous diet in summer. Some of the insect eaters will not come to bird feeders, but others respond well to suet, suet mixes, bakery products, fruits, softened raisins, and—best of all, if we go to the trouble of visiting a bait store—mealworms. Whatever their diets may be, most birds will respond to the choice foods we offer in summer. And, as in winter, this may help them get safely through any emergencies.

Do birds that receive extra food from humans during the breeding season achieve better nesting success than birds that do not? This is a question that seems not to have been studied in songbirds. But in a three-year study conducted in the Florida Keys by George Powell of the National Audubon Society, it was found that great white herons provided with extra food by area residents had much better nesting success than those birds of the same species relying solely on food obtained in the wild. His study involved measuring the nesting success of great white

Certain birds, such as the three bluebird species, have benefited greatly from human assistance.

herons that got a significant portion of their diets from fish thrown them by area fishermen. When compared with herons not benefitting from these handouts, Powell found that the panhandling herons fledged an average of one additional nestling per nest. (From *Audubon Ark*, by Frank Graham, Jr. published by Alfred A. Knopf, 1990.)

It would be helpful to know through studies such as those conducted in Sweden and Wisconsin if supplementary feeding in summer significantly increases the survival chances of birds. It almost certainly does in regard to hummingbirds, but there is little available information on this subject. Perhaps those of us feeding birds today will help to provide answers to these questions for the feeding station operators of the future. □

QUICK REFERENCE
BIRD FEEDING CHART

Bird Species	Preferred Food	Readily Eaten
Quail, pheasants	Cracked corn	Millet, berries
Pigeons, doves	Millet	Sunflower, milo, bread, nuts and cracked corn
Roadrunners	Meat scraps	Suet
Hummingbirds	Plant nectar, small insects	Sugar water
Woodpeckers	Suet, meat scraps	Fruits, nuts, sunflower seed, sugar water
Jays	Peanut kernels	Sunflower (striped), suet, bread products
Crows, magpies, and nutcrackers	Meat scraps, suet	Peanuts, bread products, dog food
Titmice, chickadees	Peanut kernels, black oil sunflower	Sunflower (striped), peanut butter, suet
Nuthatches, creepers	Suet, suet mixes	Sunflower seed, nuts, cracked corn, breads
Wrens	Suet, suet mixes	Peanut butter, nut meats, bread, apple
Mockingbirds, thrashers	Halved apple, fruits	Bread products, suet, sunflower seeds, nuts
Robins, bluebirds, and other thrushes	Suet pieces, mealworms, berries, water	Bread products, raisins, currants, nut meats
Kinglets	Suet, suet mixes	Bread products
Waxwings	Berries, raisins	Sliced apple, canned peas, currants
Warblers	Suet, suet mixes, water	Fruits, breads, sugar water, nut pieces
Tanagers	Suet, fruits	Sugar water, mealworms, breads
Cardinals, grosbeaks, buntings	Sunflower seed	Safflower, apple, other fruits, suet, millet, breads
Towhees, juncos	Millet, sunflower	Cracked corn, peanuts, breads, nut meats

Bird Species	Preferred Food	Readily Eaten
Sparrows	Millet, peanut kernels	Bread crumbs, canary seed, sunflower, suet
Blackbirds, Starlings	Cracked corn, milo Scraps, bread, suet	Millet, suet, bread Cracked corn, nutmeats
Orioles	Sugar water, fruit pieces	Jelly, suet, softened raisins, orange pieces
Finches	Thistle (niger) seed, black oil sunflower	Hulled sunflower seed, millet, fruits, suet mixes, peanuts

Important Bird Feeding Facts

When buying seed: *Black oil* sunflower seed is greatly preferred by most birds to white-striped sunflower seed. *White proso* millet is greatly preferred to red millet.

Wild bird seed mixes may include large percentages of "filler" materials not readily eaten by birds. The best economy is to create your own mix or use only black oil sunflower seed.

When offering suet, outside temperatures of above 75 degrees F. may turn suet rancid which can be dangerous for birds. Replace your suet regularly, or don't offer it on warm days.

Where the listing "fruits" appears in the chart above it is meant to include any of the following: Sliced apples, oranges, bananas, melons, as well as grapes, raisins, and currants.

Water is another way to attract birds to your yard. During winter, an unfrozen source of water will be welcomed by birds.

Sugar water mixtures should be *four parts water to one part sugar*. Sweeter mixtures are not more attractive to birds, and may even be dangerous for them. *Never use honey.*

This chart is intended as a general guideline for bird feeding. You may find that certain foods listed above are not readily consumed by the birds at your feeders, or that some foods not listed above are more eagerly eaten. These seeds and food types reflect the current feeding practices, and our knowledge about what attracts birds to our feeders.

The best way to attract birds is to landscape your yard with shrubs, trees, and flowering plants which naturally will provide food and shelter. Each regional chapter of this book offers some suggestions for such plantings. For more suggestions, contact a local landscaper, greenhouse, or your local agricultural extension agent. Remember it is best to use native species, as well as exotics, when landscaping your property.

See the charts on pages 184-185 for a listing of plants which provide food and shelter for birds

Fruit-bearing Trees and Shrubs for Birds

Common Name	Botanical Name	Regions
Strawberry Tree	*Arbutus unedo*	Calif., Pacific NW
Manzanita	*Arctostaphylos spp.*	Calif., Pacific NW, Gr. Basin
Hackberry	*Celtis spp.*	Gr. Plains, S. Texas, Southwest
Dogwood	*Cornus spp.*	Gr. Plains, Rockies, Gr. Basin, Calif., Pacific NW
Cotoneaster	*Cotoneaster spp.*	Gr. Plains, Rockies, Gr. Basin, Calif., Pacific NW
Russian Olive Autumn Olive	*Elaeagnus spp.*	Gr. Plains, Rockies, Gr. Basin
Loquat	*Eriobotrya japonica*	S. Texas, Southwest, S. Calif.
Toyon	*Heteromeles arbutifolia*	Southwest, S. Calif.
Holly	*Ilex spp.*	Gr. Plains, Southwest, Calif., Pacific NW
Oregon Grape	*Mahonia aquifolium*	Calif., Pacific NW
Flowering Crab Apple	*Malus floribunda* (*var. Hopa*)	Gr. Plains, Southwest, Rockies, Gr. Basin, Calif., Pacific NW
Nandina	*Nandina domestica*	S. Texas, Southwest, Calif., Pacific NW
Pyracantha	*Pyracantha coccinea* (*var. Lalandei*)	All regions
Japanese Rose	*Rosa multiflora*	Gr. Plains, Gr. Basin
Blue Elderberry	*Sambucus glauca*	Calif., Pacific NW
Chinese Tallow Tree	*Sapium sebiferum*	S. Texas, Southwest, S. Calif.
California Pepper Tree	*Schinus molle*	Southwest, S. Calif.
Buffalo Berry	*Shepherdia spp.*	N. Gr. Plains, Rockies, Gr. Basin
Mountain Ash	*Sorbus spp.*	N. Gr. Plains, Rockies, Gr. Basin, Pacific NW
Snow Berry	*Symphoricarpos albus*	N. Gr. Plains, Rockies, Gr. Basin, Pacific NW

Plants for Hummingbirds

Common Name	Botanical Name	Regions
Silk Tree, Mimosa	*Albizia julibrissin*	S. Gr. Plains, S. Texas, Southwest, S. Calif.
American Columbine	*Aquilegia canadensis*	Gr. Plains, Rockies, Pacific NW
Common Butterfly Bush	*Buddleia davidii*	S. Gr. Plains, Southwest, Calif.
Trumpet Creeper	*Campsis radicans*	Gr. Plains, Southwest, Calif., Pacific NW
Flowering Quince	*Chaenomeles spp.*	Gr. Plains, Southwest, Gr. Basin, Calif., Pacific NW
Scarlet Larkspur	*Delphinium cardinale*	Southwest, Calif.
Fuchsia	*Fuchsia spp*	Calif., Pacific NW
Coralbells	*Heuchera sanguinea*	Gr. Plains, Southwest, Calif., Pacific NW
Shrimp plant	*Justicia brandegeana*	S. Texas, Southwest
Trumpet Honeysuckle	*Lonicera sempervirens*	Gr. Plains, Rockies, Gr. Basin, Calif., Pacific NW
Monkeyflower	*Mimulus cardinalis*	Southwest, Calif., Pacific NW
Bee Balm	*Monarda didyma*	Gr. Plains, Rockies, Gr. Basin, Calif., Pacific NW
Beardtongue, Scarlet Bugler	*Penstemon cardinalis*	S. Texas, Southwest, Calif.
Autumn Sage Garden Sage, Mexican Sage Pineapple Sage, Scarlet Sage	*Salvia spp.*	One or more sages suitable for every region
Cape Honeysuckle	*Tecomaria capensis*	S. Texas, Southwest, S. Calif.

Index